Black's Picture Sports

Trout Fishing

Black's Picture Sports

Trout Fishing

David Sceats

Adam and Charles Black · London

First published 1982 by A & C Black (Publishers) Ltd,
35 Bedford Row, London WC1R 4JH
ISBN 0-7136-2111-7

Sceats, David
Trout fishing. – (Black's picture sports)
1. Trout fishing   2. Fly fishing
I. Title
799.1′755   SH687

ISBN 0–7136–2111–7

Line drawings by Christine Gilbert
Photos 1–13, 18, 20 by Andrew Franks
14 by Donald Shell
15–17, 19 by Robert Fry
21–47 by Clive Collier

Typeset by King's English Typesetters Ltd, Cambridge
Printed by J. W. Arrowsmith Ltd, Bristol

Contents

A young angler fishing a small private lake.

A typical small private day ticket water of the sort recommended by the author for beginners to start their fishing.

Introduction

Fly fishing is a form of hunting; to be successful at it you need to grasp before you start that this means using your powers of observation, reason and skill to outwit a wild creature in its own world. This book has been written with this idea in mind, and you will miss the point if you don't realise that going fishing challenges you to pit your wits against those of the fish in a kind of hand to hand combat. If *you* don't get the better of *it* you will come home empty-handed.

In this book, I have tried to follow the logic of the hunt, asking first what it is about trout that makes it possible for us to catch them in the first place. This means looking at how fish live, the world they live in, and at what they eat; and then at how you can persuade them to try and eat the artificial fly on the end of your line, for if the fish never try to eat the fly you won't get very far with catching them. Once you understand what you are trying to do in fly fishing, then is the time to think about how to do it and what equipment you will need.

Fish spend the vast bulk of their active lives in the search for food, and it is likely, therefore, that your best chance of catching them will be to offer them something which resembles what they are eating – artificial flies that represent the insects on which you might reasonably expect them to be feeding. Such imitative flies are generally fairly easy to tie yourself, and dressing and using your own flies is an essential part of fly fishing; it brings you into such close contact with the 'business end' of your tackle and the world of the trout. Any would-be fly-fisher ought to begin to tie flies as soon as possible in his fishing career, and to help you start I have included a brief chapter on basic fly-dressing.

Many different kinds of fish can be caught with artificial flies, but I have written only about trout because they are the quarry you are most likely to be after. But why fish with the fly at all? After all, trout can be caught with bait – what's the attraction in using a fly?

Most obviously there is the difference in approach: the bait fisherman offers the fish something actually edible with a hook concealed in it, while the fly fisherman offers it a hook disguised to look like one of the insects that form its natural diet. This means that fly fishing is almost always more exciting and satisfying than bait fishing because it depends so much more on the skill of the fisherman in *deceiving* the fish. In bait fishing it is the sheer edibility of the bait that makes the fish seize it; in fly fishing it is the fisherman's skill in deceiving the fish into taking a few wisps of fur and feather for a living fly or pupa.

Another attraction is that the fly-fisher is much more likely to be fishing for a specific fish – especially if he is lucky enough to be fishing a stream – because feeding trout tend to give away where they are by displacing water in a 'rise'. And this brings us back to where we began: the challenge of personal combat with the trout is simply so much more obvious when you cast to a particular fish that you have watched and stalked in order to do so. Fishing is hunting – and fly fishing is you *versus* the trout.

1 The Trout and its World

Fly-fishing is possible for the simple reason that trout eat insects, and in order to do so they must obviously get hold of them with their mouths. Of course, once a trout gets hold of an *artificial* insect with its mouth it soon realises its mistake and spits it out again, but provided we can get it to take our fly into its mouth in the first place, we have just long enough to set the hook by striking with the rod (see p. 67) before the fly is ejected, and so we can catch the fish. So far as we know, of course, trout are not really capable of *thinking;* their minds work by instinct and their actions are not the result of a process of reasoning but responses triggered off by circumstances. However, they are obviously very capable of learning from experience, and you won't go far wrong if you regard them as thinking creatures! Much better to overestimate your quarry's abilities than to underestimate them.

There are two instincts in particular which you must be aware of as a fisherman: hunger and self-preservation. The fisherman's aim is to trigger the first without triggering the second, and to be able to do that we must first know something about the trout and its behaviour in its own world.

HOW TROUT SEE

Like people, trout have five senses, but there are two which are especially important for our purposes – sight and hearing. Sight is the more important for feeding because by it the fish decides what to try and eat. All sorts of things may come drifting down the current of a stream or be blown onto the surface of a lake – leaves, twigs, cigarette ends, and so on as well as edible things like worms and insects. When something that looks edible comes into the view of a feeding fish, it may stimulate a very swift response, or the fish may have a closer look before seizing (or leaving) the object in question, but if it decides to eat it, it sucks it in by opening its mouth and gills together, making the water immediately in front of it rush in through its mouth carrying the item of food with it; it can very easily reverse the process if it dislikes the feel or taste of the item, by closing the gills and so forcing the water (with the object) out again. The large size of the gills compared with the relatively small area of the mouth means that it can eject unwanted items very quickly and this, in turn, means that you have not long in which to set the hook when the item in question happens to be your artificial fly.

Trout see other things as well as potential food. They see, for instance, their enemies, including fishermen, and though they may not stop feeding just because they see you, especially if you are beyond their range of focus at the time, they are likely to become jittery, and therefore harder to catch; and if you get too close, they will take fright and swim away at high speed, so both from the point of view of deceiving them, and from that of not scaring them, it is important to know something about *how* trout see things.

The position of the trout's eyes in its head means that it sees most easily upwards and forwards, rather than downwards or backwards, and this means that it tends to swim about at a level in the water below that at which its main food supply is to be found, looking ahead and upwards and rising in the water when it sees something to eat. But its vision is not limited by the surface of the water. Figure 1 shows how the trout sees upward: the physical properties of light have the effect of making

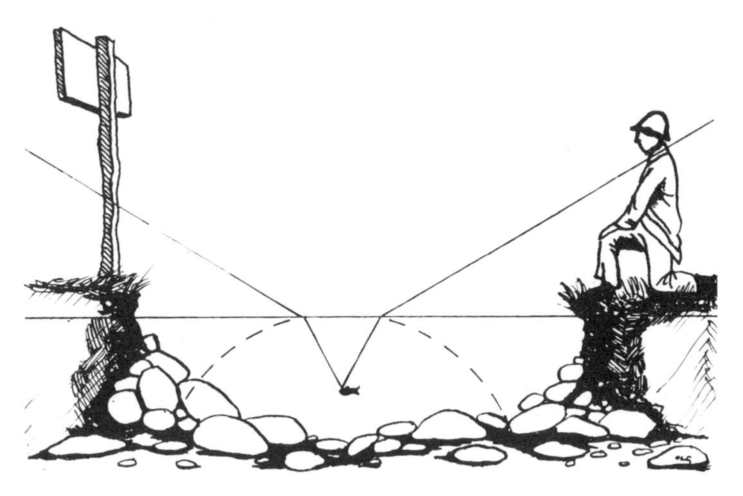

Figure 1a How the trout sees out of the water.

b What the trout sees through its 'window'.

most of the surface of the water into a mirror, which appears to slope downwards all round, reflecting the bottom and the things in the water, except for a circular area immediately over the fish, called its 'window', through which it sees into the world beyond the water. The calmer the water the better both the picture of the underwater world in the 'mirror', and the view of the world beyond the surface. If the water is ruffled by wind or current both the 'mirror' and the 'window' become distorted. Figure 1 also shows the results from the trout's point of view of the fact that light 'bends' when it enters water, which means that the fish can see more through the 'window' than you would expect, though objects which are low down and consequently near the edge of the 'window' are distorted and indistinct. Under the surface, provided the water is clear, the fish can see comparatively far, but the less light that penetrates, due to mud particles in suspension, overhanging trees, increased depth and so on, the more restricted its distance vision becomes. Moreover, there is a blind spot of about 30 degrees behind its head, so if you know which way it is facing, you can approach with less chance of being seen.

All this has some obvious results; the lower you keep in the fish's field of vision, the less likely you are to scare it, and you are also less likely to 'put it down' if you avoid drawing attention to yourself by sudden movements, or

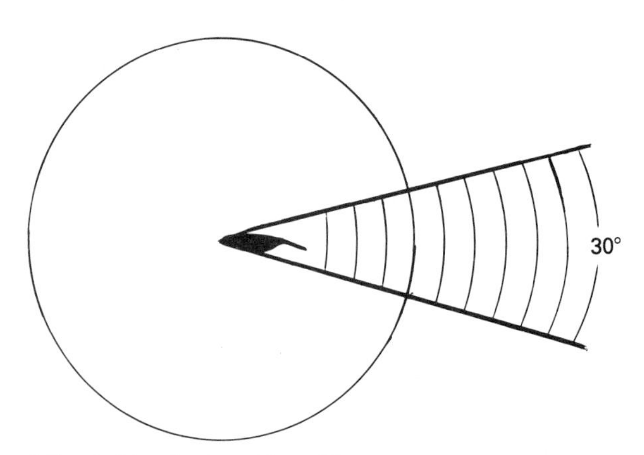

Figure 2 Trout vision back and front. The shaded area is the fish's 'blind spot'.

An angler making use of the bankside vegetation as cover from a rising trout. Note how the back-cast is being made with the rod horizontal to avoid tangling the fly on the bushes.

The angler using the bank as cover by 'hiding' in front of his background.

by wearing bright or light coloured clothing. In fact, providing you wear something dull and basically greenish or brownish, and avoid being seen by the fish against the skyline, you will be able to get quite close without being seen at all. The use of background is important too: it is better to hide from trout *in front* of something than behind it, providing your clothes merge with the scenery; a trout will see you much better against the skyline formed by the edges of bushes and trees than against the background of the bushes and trees themselves. Wading is another way of keeping low in its field of view, though, as we shall see, there are other problems when you get in the water, and if you are fishing lakes you should avoid wading as far as possible because it scares fish out of the shallow margins. If you observe these precautions you will find you can often get within 15 or 20 yards of a trout without 'putting it down', and on streams where the fish lie head-to-current you can get even closer by approaching from downstream.

THE TROUT'S SENSE OF HEARING

From the point of view of the trout, hearing is probably as important as sight for self-preservation, especially from anglers! Actually, it's not so much hearing in our sense of the word as sensitivity to vibration. Trout are not aware of the high-frequency vibrations we call sounds, so you will not disturb them (though you may upset your fellow-fishermen) by cursing loudly when you catch a tree on the back-cast. But they are highly sensitive to low-frequency vibrations – shakes and shocks – both in the water and on the surrounding banks. Anything which sends vibrations through the water will drive them far out of casting range. On a stream you may upset a whole beat by frightening fish in one spot, because they will swim away upstream and communicate their nervousness to undisturbed fish above them.

Again, the implications are obvious. You must at all costs avoid any of the following: falling in the water, kicking lumps of the bank into the water, stumping about on the bank, splashing or creating waves while wading, banging on the bottom of boats or making them rock in the water, and splashing the line down when casting. When wading try to move without disturbing the water, and always wait several moments after entering a stream before you start moving or fishing. Wading is safer in streams provided you fish from downstream, since the current carries much of the disturbance away from the fish, but you can still send shock-waves upstream against the current; in lakes where there is no current you should avoid wading as much as possible.

TROUT BEHAVIOUR IN LAKES

Lake trout lack the basic advantage of river trout: there is no current bringing them a continuous supply of food, and so they must spend most of their time swimming about looking for it. All sorts of factors to do with the weather, water conditions and the shape of the bottom of the lake will influence their precise position, but in general they will be where the food is most plentiful, and since most of the insects on which trout feed live among weeds in relatively shallow water (up to about 20 feet), they can usually be found fairly near the banks. However, food is not the only determining factor: the temperature of the water is also important. If the water is extremely cold trout find it uncomfortable, whereas if it warms up beyond a certain point they need increasing amounts of oxygen to be active, while the amount of oxygen dissolved in the water decreases with increasing temperature. So in very cold and very warm weather the fish avoid the shallows, and in the early part of the season and in high summer they are often in rather deeper water. In lakes where wading is allowed anglers often wade unthinkingly as deep as they can, and this has the effect of both driving the fish out of the shallow margins, and of destroying the underwater vegetation where the insects live on which the trout feed, and thus reducing the likelihood that trout will be found near the bank.

Nevertheless, in general fish can be expected to congregate around weed beds and in any places where the bottom gives them extra cover, so they are likely to be near submerged tree stumps, roots, holes and banks (see Figure 3). They also gather, for some reason, near submerged roads, in reservoirs which have been formed by flooding valleys. Another likely place, especially at the end of the season, is where inflow streams enter the lake, since brown trout would naturally move into the feeder streams in September to begin the search for a place to spawn. They often feed in the area where ripples begin beyond the flat water under the windward shore of a lake, partly because there, where the wind meets the water, insects will be blown down onto the surface, and when the wind is strong they will sometimes lie facing it in the upper layers of the water which are being moved by the wind, much as a river trout will lie head-to-current. Even where none of these factors apply, it is not unusual to find particular fish 'patrolling' a 'beat' along a weed-bed or some other underwater feature, and giving away its presence by regular rises; careful observation can often lead to the capture of such a fish by putting a fly in the water where you know it is likely to rise next.

TROUT BEHAVIOUR IN STREAMS

In streams everything is governed by the current: the trout has no need to go looking for food since the current brings it, and fish are, therefore, relatively stationary for quite long periods while feeding, and will often feed in the same spot in the stream from day to day (unless they are caught!) Keeping in the same place in a strong current obviously requires a constant expenditure of energy, however, and is only worthwhile if the energy consumed is more than made up by the food which the current supplies. So in practice fish will lie out of the main flow in some kind of shelter – under the bank,

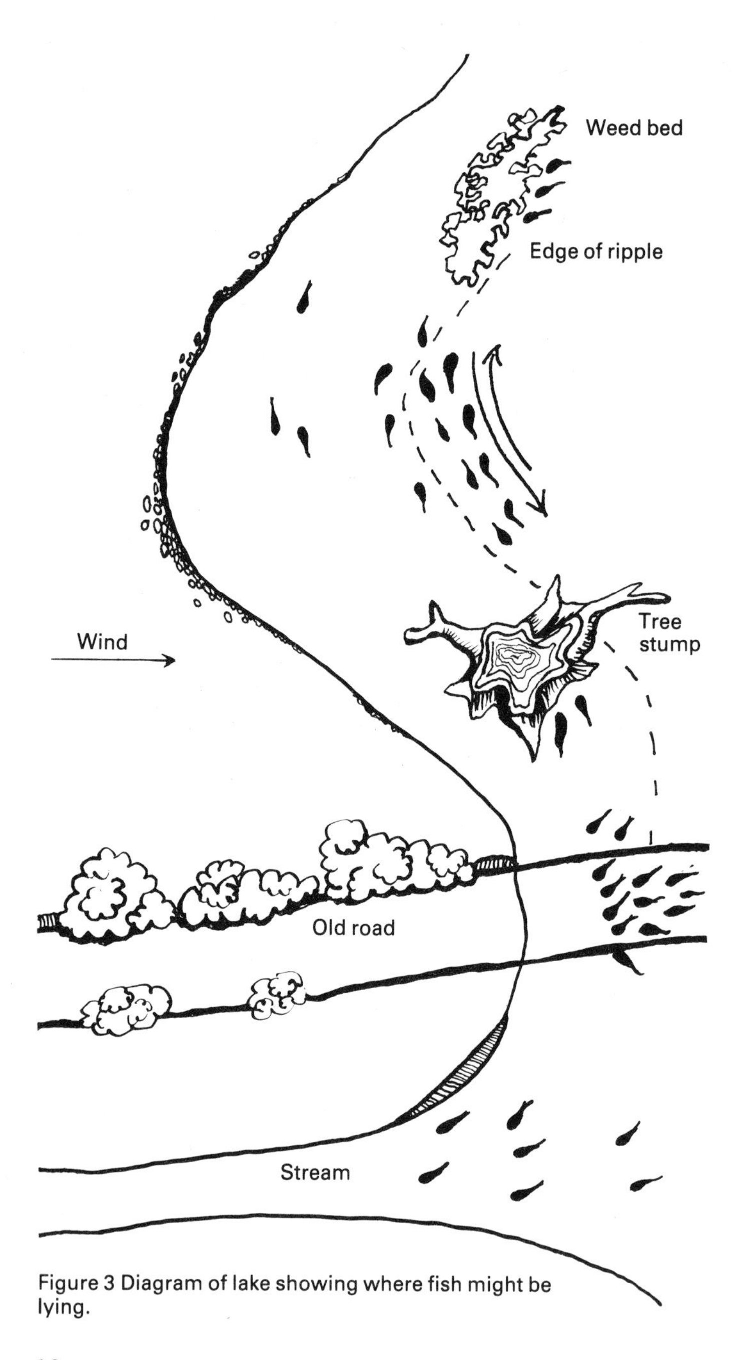

Figure 3 Diagram of lake showing where fish might be lying.

behind boulders and rocks, where tree-roots break the current, and in back eddies, for instance – where they can keep an eye on the food supply and slip out to grab it with minimum effort. Naturally they face upstream, and their attention is focussed forwards and upwards: in this way they can both see the food supply as the current brings it (either on the surface or in mid-water), and the flow of water over their gills allows them to breathe. Fish in lakes must keep moving to achieve this latter result.

The question of food supply also governs whereabouts in the stream trout are likely to be concentrated. As with lake trout, stream fish will be more numerous where there is more to eat, and since their food is brought to them on the current, they will gather in places in the stream where the current will bring the most food. Anywhere that the current is funnelled and food may be swept along is a likely spot to find fish; such places are the channels between weed beds, the tails of pools, places where the current sets into one bank at a bend, or where

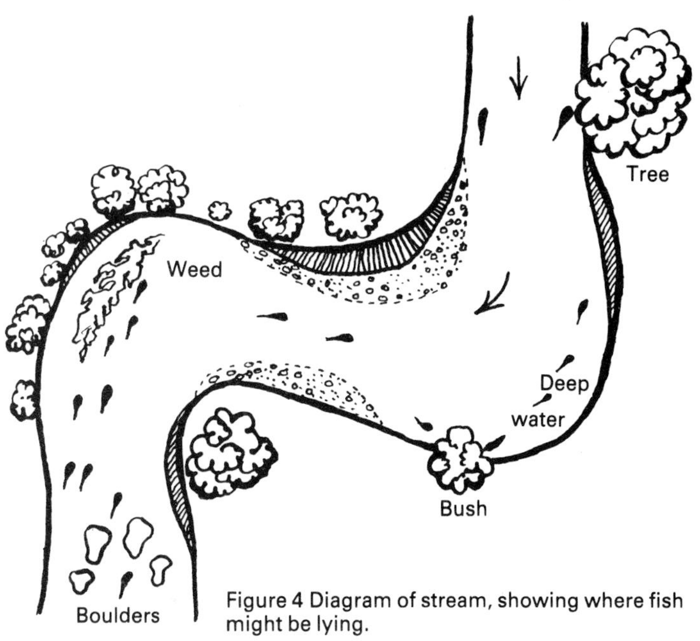

Figure 4 Diagram of stream, showing where fish might be lying.

the main flow is constricted into a narrow passage between shingle beds or islands. Often such places afford cover as well as refreshments and so are doubly likely to be fishy places (Figure 4).

Because streams are generally much shallower than lakes, trout in them more often reveal their presence by 'rising'. A rise is a swirl or boil on the surface caused either by a fish actually coming up to take fly off the surface, or by fish below the surface moving suddenly to seize an insect in mid-water and displacing water above it which shows as a swirl at the surface a moment later, and can often be heard as well as seen. Rises, therefore, do not necessarily mean fish feeding at the surface, though it's generally possible to tell by watching them whether a fish is actually coming up. Obviously the deeper the fish the quieter and less splashy the rise will be; on the other hand fish sometimes come up to the surface and sip at dead or dying flies that are on it, and these rises can be very delicate, so that quietness does not always mean a fish feeding in mid-water. But the deeper the fish the longer the displaced water will take to reach the surface, and if you *hear* a rise rather than seeing it, it will have moved downstream on the current by the time your eyes pick it up, so rises commonly show themselves downstream of the fish's position, and to cast to the fish that caused them you will need to allow for this.

THE TIME OF THE RISE

The fact that no fish are rising does not mean none are feeding. It merely suggests they are feeding at a depth at which the displaced water is dissipated before reaching the surface in a rise. This is the situation for most of the time on lakes, and for some of the time on streams, and when no rises are to be seen there is little point in fishing water which you know to be so shallow that a feeding fish must give itself away. On the other hand there are times when both lake and stream seem to come alive with rising fish. These times, known simply as 'the rise', are often quite predictable, for they result from sudden increases in insect activity which are, in turn, associated with stages in the life cycles of the insects trout feed on, and with external factors like air and water temperature, wind speed, and so on. In general you can expect the rise in the early part of the season to be in the middle of the day, between about 12.30 and 2.30 pm; from early June onwards this gradually gives way to a late afternoon rise around 5.30 to 8.00 pm; often followed by an evening rise as dusk falls, and, (especially in the case of lakes) when the wind drops and the evening calm begins. From mid-July to the end of August the main rises are around dusk and dawn, while in September the midday rise gradually reappears. It is thus often possible to plan your fishing to meet the rise, and so avoid spending fruitless and frustrating hours by the waterside. But trout are not machines, so do not be surprised if they decide not to perform to order.

2 The Natural Fly

If we need to know something about the lifestyle of the fish to catch it with a fly, we obviously need as well to know something about the flies which trout eat. Of course, flies are not the only things trout eat. There are recorded instances of them being caught with frogs and even water rats in their stomachs, and I once saw a sea-trout caught by a roach-fisherman, on a piece of stewed wheat. But as fly fishermen, our concern is with the major portion of the trout's diet – insects of various kinds which live and breed in the water.

Most of the insects we are concerned with begin their life as eggs, somewhere near the bottom of the lake or stream, which hatch out into an immature underwater insect, usually called either a *nymph* or a *pupa*. These insects live on or near the bottom for a period varying from weeks to over a year, usually in a weed bed which provides shelter and nourishment. As the time for transformation into the adult insect draws near, most of these nymphs begin to swim about more freely in midwater, eventually ascending to the surface. There a startling transformation takes place. The insect sheds its skin, and out of the wingless, swimming, underwater-breathing nymph, emerges a winged, air-breathing fly which flutters away into the air. Most of these flies live only a short time – sometimes a mere matter of hours – and the one purpose of their existence is to find a mate. When they have done so, the female flies return to the water

A typical weed bed in a stream providing shelter and food for a wide variety of insects.

surface and lay their eggs, which sink to the bottom, and then they die, remaining trapped in the surface film until they are eaten or sink themselves. See Figure 5.

FISHING THE FLY

There are four times during this process when insects are particularly exposed to the attentions of fish: in the period before hatching when the nymphs are ascending to the surface; at the moment of hatching itself, when the fly is struggling to release itself both from its nymphal skin and from the surface tension of the water (which can be quite difficult on lakes when the water is glassy-calm, and insects get trapped on the underside of the surface, which makes them very vulnerable); during the period when the hatched fly (called a dun) sits on the surface to dry its wings before taking off; and when the females (called spinners) return to the water to lay their eggs and die. Obviously your best chance of deceiving the fish will

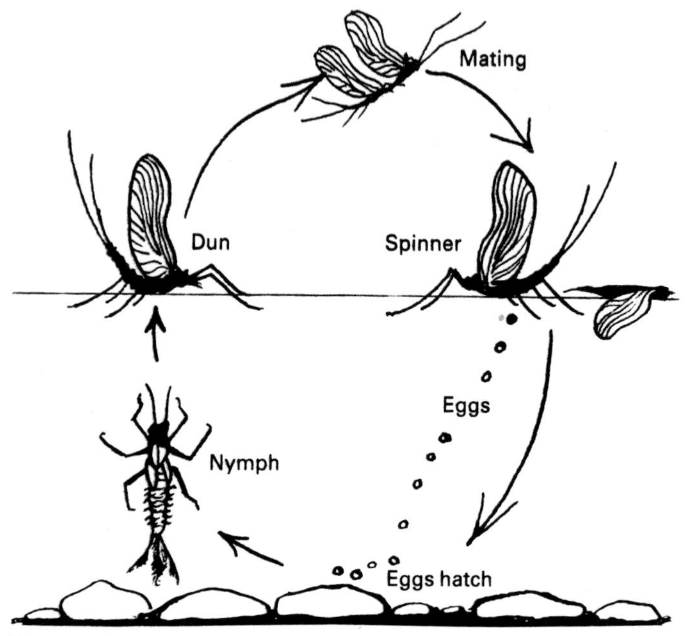

Figure 5 Life cycle of fly.

be to imitate the fly in one or other of these stages; to do that you will have to come to two decisions: which fly to choose and which stage to imitate.

Actually this is not nearly so difficult as it sounds. Artificial flies are not usually exact *copies* of natural insects. They are *imitations*, and they work because something about them – size, colour, outline, the way they sit on the water – triggers the feeding instinct of the trout. It is possible, therefore, to imitate a number of similar insects of the same type with one or two 'general' fly patterns for each crucial stage of the life-cycle; most artificial flies are designed to resemble one or other of these stages (see Figure 6). There are two basic types of artificial: those fished under the surface, generally called 'nymphs' by fishermen, and those fished on the surface, known as 'dry flies'. On the lake, nymphs are much the more important of the two, but on the stream the two types are of more or less equal usefulness.

Natural midge pupa

Artificial midge pupa

Figure 6 Natural and artificial flies. The artificial emphasises the bulky thorax, the breathing tubes and the segmented body of the natural.

NATURAL FLIES OF STILLWATER

Lakes and streams each have their own different population of insects. In lakes the most important type is the family of *midges*, sometimes known to fishermen as 'buzzers'. Huge numbers are always present in lakes of all sizes and they constitute up to 80% of the diet of lake trout. But midges hatch very quickly from the surface, and though they return to the water as spinners in the evening, your best chance of catching fish with them will be with an imitation of the pupa. Midge pupae live on or near the bottom for most of their lives; when the time comes for them to hatch they swim more or less directly to the surface (though they never move at all quickly) without hanging about in midwater. However, they often get stuck in the surface film, especially in the calm evening conditions they favour for hatching, and if large numbers are coming up to the surface this can lead to a very vigorous rise by the trout, which take the pupae with a slow head and tail roll which is quite unmistakable.

Conveniently from our point of view, midge pupae are hook-shaped (Figure 7). They vary in length from about ¼in to ¾in, and their colours are also very varied; most

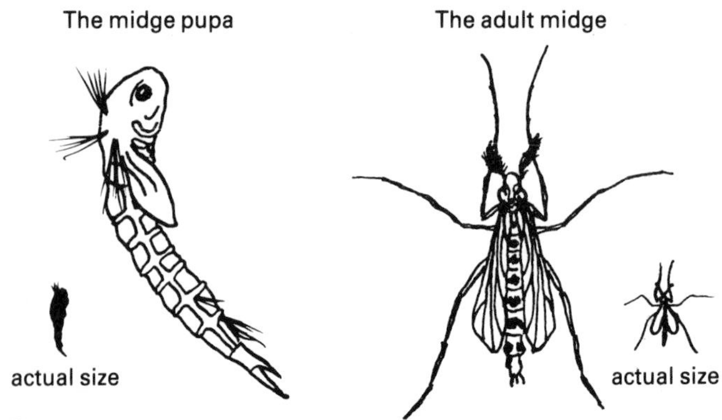

Figure 7

common are red, green, black, brown and amber. Midges of different kinds hatch at all times of day and on all days throughout the season, but they only provoke a definite rise when they appear in quantity, which is mainly in the calm conditions of early morning or late evening. The table at the end of the chapter shows the main varieties with the periods during the season when they are likely to hatch.

Next in importance to the midges are the *sedge flies*, (Figure 8) which flutter like moths over the surface of the water on summer evenings. Sedges begin to appear in June and continue throughout the season, and they are eaten by the trout in both the pupal stage as they ascend to hatch, and as adults, scuttering about the surface. But

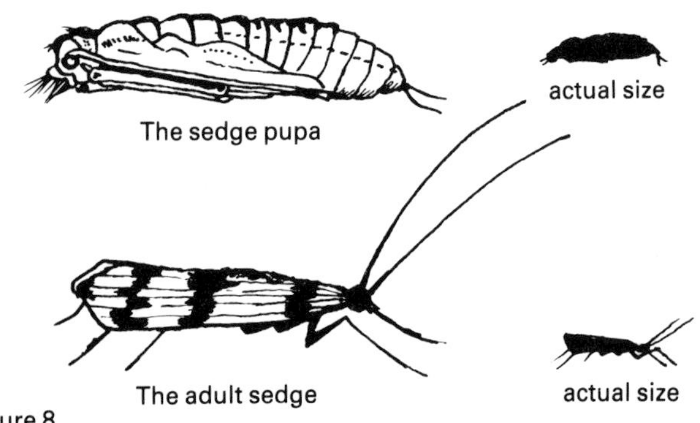

Figure 8

most of their life is spent as larvae, or caddis, in a 'shell' or case which they construct from bits of grit, leaves and twigs. Eventually the pupae leave their cases and ascend to the surface to become adult flies, moving somewhat faster in the water than midge pupae do. As with the midges, the pupal stage does not last long, but does involve large numbers of insects. Sedges may swim some distance before hatching, and though hatches may take place at any time of day or night, they are usually most active around dusk. You can tell when a hatch has begun by the sudden appearance of quantities of the adult flies, with their long feelers and fluttering wings. The main colours of both pupa and fly are amber, brown, green and greyish-yellow and their length varies from ½in to 1in.

The least important large group of flies on stillwater is, surprisingly, the most important on rivers – the *olives* – but though they form only a small part of the food eaten by lake trout they matter to fishermen because their nymphs are active in midwater for longer periods than the pupae of midges and sedges. They can also swim relatively fast for short distances. All the flies of this group which you need be concerned with are of similar size, about ⅓in long, and again the nymphs are more important than the duns or spinners. They hatch out of eggs and swim about in the water for weeks or months

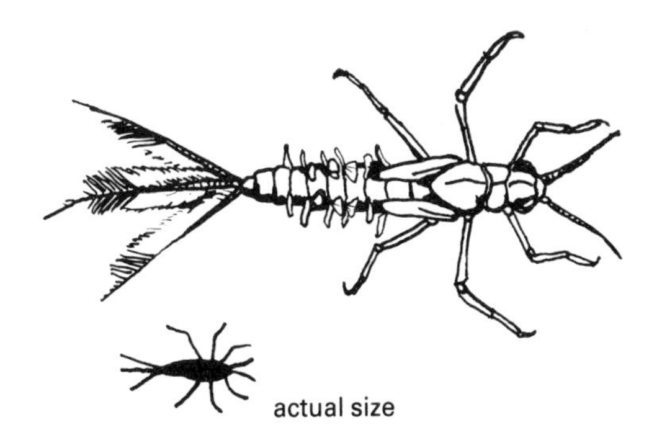

Figure 9 The olive nymph.

before ascending to hatch, and have a distinctive hump-backed appearance, three short tails, and are usually greenish-brown in colour (Figure 9).

NATURAL FLIES OF THE STREAM

The two main groups of flies which fishermen imitate on streams are olives and sedges, both of which we have just met. *Sedges* in running water behave much the way of those in still water; the only difference is due to the all-embracing influence of the current: obviously any pupa or nymph ascending to hatch moves not only upwards, but downstream as the current takes hold of it, and the same applies to flies on the surface. As we shall see, this has important consequences for presentation: it makes dry-fly fishing much more possible on streams than on lakes, but at the same time it makes nymph fishing rather trickier, since no natural nymph can swim against the full force of the current, and you must make your artificial nymph behave in as natural a way as possible. On the stream the adult sedge is certainly a more important fly from the fisherman's standpoint than the pupa.

Olives, on the other hand, are a much bigger proposition on the stream than on the lake. For a start there are so many more of them, and the precise kinds vary from stream to stream; they are, in fact, the running water equivalent of midges in lakes. Their life-cycle follows the general pattern on page 24, except that they have two adult stages: the nymphs first hatch into duns, which fly off to nearby bushes, and there moult their skins again to become spinners which mate, and the females return to lay their eggs. Flies of this type are active throughout the season, but, like the midges, each variety has a short season of its own. There is not much point, at this stage, in trying to master the names and peculiarities of them all, especially since there are a number of 'general purpose' artificials that, in a range of sizes, will serve as imitations of a number of different olives, and it is these

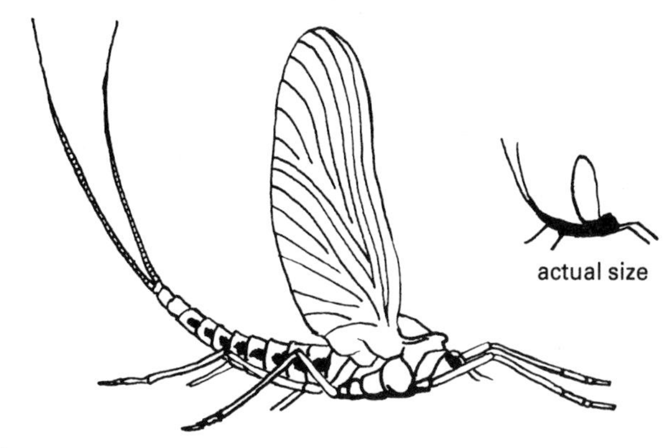

Figure 10 The olive adult.

flies which, as far as possible, I shall be recommending you to use. What is important, however, is to have some idea what size and colour you may expect the natural olives on the water to be at various stages in the season.

Apart from the mayfly, which I will describe in a moment, the olives vary between about ¼in and ½in, and, in general the earlier the season, the larger and darker the fly, in both nymphal and adult stages (Figure 10). The suggestions I made in the last chapter about the time of the rise apply also to the hatch of these flies, since it is the hatch which causes the rise, and when the flies are on the water, you must simply try to match your artificial to the size and colour of the natural insects. When the flies are not in evidence, or the trout are not rising, you should fish one of the nymph patterns I shall suggest in the next chapter in a size appropriate to the season. The only modification to these 'rules' is that in September the natural flies grow bigger again, and also darker, so repeating the pattern of the beginning of the season.

At the end of May, on some streams, the mayfly appears, and the trout go crazy. Mayflies are huge olives, an inch or more long, and they look bigger because of their light colour and long tails. They are a creamy off-white shade, with long fat bodies, and the trout love

them; even big cannibal fish that live in the deep pools and feed only on shrimps and worms and the offspring of their own cousins will come up to the surface in mayfly time! The mayfly season usually lasts two or three weeks, during which the trout gorge themselves on nymphs, duns and spinners, and it is often followed by a week or so in which they are lethargic and unresponsive to anything you throw at them – presumably because of the after-effects of their banquet. Fishermen who have a mayfly hatch on their water are generally regarded as very lucky by their less fortunate comrades, and there are few experiences in fishing quite so exciting as the evening spinner-fall when the air is thick with mayflies falling like gigantic snowflakes on the water, and the trout are rising all over the stream as though feeding was about to go out of fashion. I need hardly add that the fact that every trout in the river is seizing live mayflies as fast as it can swallow them need not make it any easier to get them to accept your artificial!

There are about eleven varieties of olive that will be present in most streams through the season, and in some there will be a good many more. I have listed the commoner ones, with their sizes and seasons in the table at the end of the chapter. Besides these, and the other insects I have described, there are a variety of others which are eaten by trout in lakes and streams, which I have not attempted to cover in this introductory book. If you want to find out more about them I suggest you look at some of the books on the subject of flies in the reading list on p. 95. What I have covered here are the insects which account for the great bulk of the trout's annual diet, and you now know enough about them to give you the chance to make a selection of an artificial fly which has every reasonable chance of imitating what the fish are actually eating.

Association water on a typical lowland trout brook. The fishing here is restricted to dry fly and upstream fishing.

Month	Lake Flies	Artificials
April	Orange-silver Midge	Orange-silver midge pupa (10-12)
	Green Midge	Green midge pupa (12)
	Pond Olive	Palmer nymph (12) Pheasant-tail nymph (12-14) Olive nymph (12)
May	Orange-silver Midge	Orange-silver midge pupa (10-14)
	Black Midge	Black midge pupa (10-14)
	Green Midge	Green midge pupa (10-12)
	Large Green Midge	Olive midge pupa (12)
	Red Midge	Orange-silver midge pupa (10-14)
	Pond Olive	As for April
	Great Red Sedge	Sedge pupa (12)
June	Orange-silver Midge	Orange-silver midge pupa (12-14)
	Green Midge	Green midge pupa (12)
	Black Midge	Black midge pupa (12-14)
	Brown Midge	Brown midge pupa (14)
	Pond Olive	Palmer nymph (12-16) Pheasant-tail nymph (14-16) Olive nymph (14-16) PVC nymph (14)
	Little Red Sedge Cinnamon Sedge	Sedge pupae (12-14) Longhorns (12-14) Invicta (12-14)
July	Green Midge	Green midge pupa (12-14)
	Black Midge	Black midge pupa (12-14)
	Red Midge	Orange-silver midge pupa (14)
	Little Brown Midge	Brown midge pupa (14)
	Golden Dun Midge	Amber midge pupa (14-16)
	Pond Olive	As for June also Light olive nymph (14)
	Red Sedge Cinnamon Sedge	As for June
August	Black Midge	Black midge pupa (12-14)
	Little Brown Midge	Brown midge pupa (14)
	Golden Dun Midge	Amber midge pupa (14-16)
	Little Green Midge	Green midge pupa (14)
	Pond Olive	Pheasant-tail nymph (16) Gold ribbed hare's ear (16) Palmer nymph (14-16) Light olive nymph (14)
	Cinnamon Sedge Caperer	As for June
September	As for August	As for August but olive nymphs in a size larger

Stream Flies	Artificials: Nymphs	Artificials: Dry Flies
March Brown Large Dark Olive	Olive nymph (12) Gold-ribbed hare's ear (12) Pheasant-tail nymph (12)	
Large Dark Olive Iron Blue (last two weeks): Blue Winged Olive Medium Olive Mayfly Great Red Sedge	Olive nymph (12-14) Pheasant-tail nymph (14-16) Gold ribbed hare's ear (14) PVC nymph (14) Mayfly nymph (10)	Imperial (14) Blue Upright (14-16) Red Quill (14) Pheasant Tail (14) Greenwell's Glory (14) Grey Duster (8-10) Brown Sedge (12)
Blue Winged Olive Medium Olive Mayfly Pale Evening Dun Olive Pale Watery Olive Little Red Sedge Cinnamon Sedge	As for May	Pheasant Tail (14) Orange Quill (14) Greenwell's Glory (14) Grey Duster (10) Spent Drake Blue Dun (14) Blue Upright (14) Grey Duster (14) Brown Sedge (12-14) Cinnamon Sedge (12)
Blue Winged Olive* Medium Olive* Pale Evening Dun Olive* Pale Watery Olive* Caenis Sedges as for June	Gold ribbed hare's ear (14-16) Palmer nymph (14-16) Light Olive nymph (14-16) Pheasant-tail nymph 14-16) PVC nymph (14-16)	Pheasant tail (14-16) Red Quill (14-16) Blue Upright (14-16) Greenwell's Glory (16) Grey Duster (18) Sedges as for June
As for July	As for July but concentrate on the smaller sizes	As for July but concentrate on the smaller sizes
Blue Winged Olive Late March Brown Dark Olive Pale Watery Olive Caperer	As for July	As for July but concentrate on the larger sizes Caperer sedge (12-14)

*July: these natural flies are capable of representation by any nymphs or dry flies shown.

3 Selecting the Artificial Fly

Fly selection is a problem in two parts. There is the question of choosing an artificial from what you have available in your fly-box, to match the natural fly in the water; there is also the question of what flies to put in the box in the first place. Obviously, the first depends on the second: what you can imitate beside the water will be determined by what you have decided to include in your box. Stocking the box can be a problem in itself, especially if you must buy your flies. A good tackle dealer will show you a huge range of flies in all sorts of attractive colours and sizes, and the temptation to buy as many different patterns as possible to give yourself the maximum chance of catching fish will be very strong.

Don't be fooled. Half those flies are there to catch fishermen! If you can afford a large number, much better get several of each of a limited number of patterns in a variety of sizes. The point is that having 30 or 40 different patterns with you does not increase your chances. It increases the likelihood of your becoming confused and unconfident. But confidence in the fly is fifty percent of successful fly-fishing. The more patterns you have in the box, the more likely you will be to put a fly on, make a cast or two without result, then pull it in and change it for another . . . and another . . . and another. Before long you will be changing flies every few casts without any *reason,* instead of thoughtfully trying to imitate the likely fly in the water. And even if you are lucky, you won't know *why*, so you won't be able to make use of your experience another time.

The way to go about filling your fly-box is to bear in mind the information about the natural flies I gave you in the last chapter: you want to provide yourself with a range of artificials that will represent the sort of flies that are common at each stage of the season on the kind of water you fish. So what flies should you have in your box? On the whole the best sort are the general or representational patterns – tied, not as copies of individual species, but to represent any fly of one type, such as olives or midges, that is of a particular size and colour. In this way you can make the maximum allowance for the variety of the natural flies while keeping to a relatively small number of tried and tested artificials; this should make for confidence in fishing. The reason confidence is so important is that the confident fisherman concentrates on what he is doing, while the unconfident concentrates on what he is afraid he isn't doing; the confident man is, therefore, much more likely to spot the signs of the fish taking his fly.

FLIES FOR THE LAKE

If your fishing is to be mainly in lakes you will need artificial midge pupae. Not every tackle dealer will know them by that name, though: you may have to ask for 'Buzzers', and if so, be careful you get the right things. Look for a fly as close as possible to that in Figure 11 and beware of patterns with names like Buzzer Nymph – they may be nothing like a midge pupa at all. The best general purpose midge pupae are black ones and green ones, closely ribbed with silver wire, which you will need in sizes 10, 12 and 14. You should also get red ones ribbed with silver lurex in sizes 10 and 12, and brown and amber, ribbed with wire, in sizes 12 and 14.

Several patterns of sedge pupae are available, and you will need them in sizes 10 and 12. I recommend Goddard's Sedge Pupa (Figure 12) in amber and brown to

Figure 11 Midge pupa pattern.

Figure 12 Sedge pupa pattern.

represent the swimming insect, and Walker's Longhorn for the hatching pupa, in green and yellow. Even better as a representation of the hatching sedge is the traditional wet-fly Invicta, fished just beneath the surface. You should have some dry sedge patterns for lake fishing too, in the same body colours and sizes as the pupae.

Patterns of olive nymphs (see Figure 13) are available in a variety of colours and shapes, giving you scope for offering the trout a range of flies when there is nothing happening at the surface. Every tackle shop will have Sawyer's Pheasant Tail Nymph in sizes 12 and 14; you will want leaded ones, which sink better in the lake. You will have more difficulty getting Mold's Olive Nymph, but it is a very good fly, and I have explained how to make it in the chapter on fly-dressing. You ought also to have Goddard's PVC Nymph and Voss Bark's Palmer Nymph in a wide range of sizes from 10 to 16. Equipped with these you will have nymphs in brown, dark and light olive, green-gold and green-brown, and you will see from the drawings that they provide a range of variations on the basic nymphal shape.

As you gain experience you may want to include in your box representations of other stillwater insects besides the ones described in the last chapter. Good imitations of corixae (lesser water boatmen), damselfly nymphs and freshwater shrimps will be available at most tackle shops, and there are also a number of effective flies which don't actually represent any insect, but look as though they ought to (by contrast with reservoir lures,

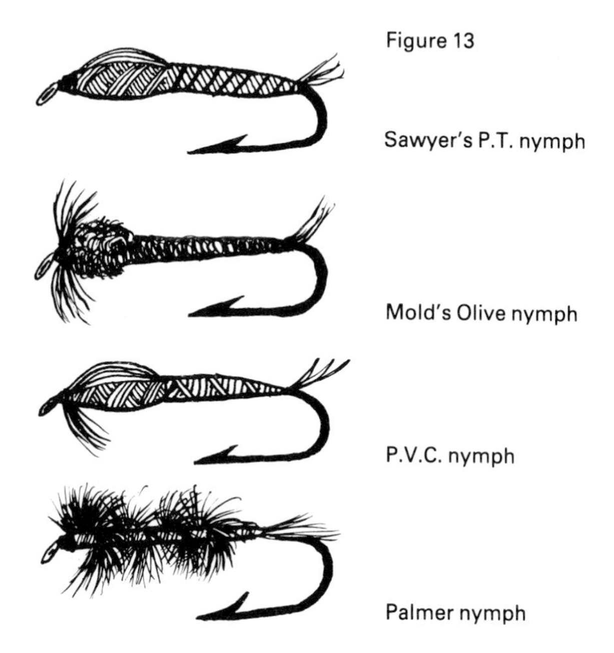

Figure 13

which look like nothing on earth). Three of the best of these are Clark's Ombudsman, Ivens' Black and Peacock Spider, and Walker's Chomper, and some of the books listed on p. 95 will tell you more about fishing them.

FLIES FOR THE STREAM

For river fishing you will need olive nymphs in size 16 as well as the larger sizes I suggested for the lake, and you should add to the list one of the best of all river nymph patterns, the Gold Ribbed Hare's Ear (Figure 14). Once again, however, you will need to be careful in buying this fly. Shop specimens are often dressed with wings and hackles like traditional wet-flies, but they are much more effective without either, and with a few strands of the body-fur straggled out like legs just behind the eye of the hook.

On streams, as on lakes, you will need sedge pupae

Figure 14 Gold ribbed hare's ear.

Figure 15 Sedge pattern.

and hatching sedges, and certainly dry sedge patterns (Figure 15). Probably the best will be Cinnamon Sedge, Brown Sedge and Little Red Sedge, in sizes 12 and 14.

Stream fishing with dry flies representing the duns and spinners of the olives is the most exciting (though not the most difficult) branch of the sport. Here more than anywhere you are well advised to go for general patterns in a range of sizes and colours when you begin. It is true that, on the chalk streams of southern England, the wild brown trout can be extremely fussy, and you may need to offer them something specifically designed to represent one species of olive; chalk stream fishers often have different patterns for the duns, spinners and spent (dead) flies of the same insect. But you are unlikely to start your fishing career in these surroundings, and, in any case, the fact that the head of trout in these waters can only be maintained by stocking fish in, means that there, as elsewhere, the fish are often less choosy.

Chalk stream trout are fussy because there is such an abundance of fly-life to choose from in their water. On limestone streams, and especially rain-fed rivers the selection is smaller and the trout readier to rise to whatever happens to be hatching, and this means you can afford to be less concerned about copying individual

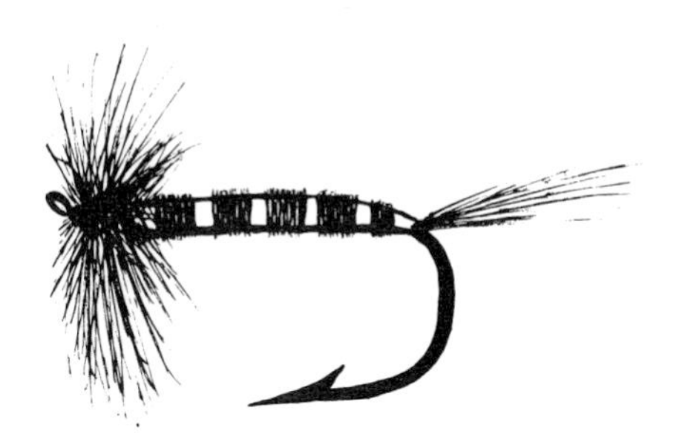

Figure 16 Hackle dry fly.

species. You must carry Pheasant Tails in sizes 14 and 16, because this very effective fly represents nearly all the olive spinners (Figure 16). Kite's Imperial in the same sizes imitates the darker duns, while Greenwell's Glory will serve for the lighter ones. The Olive Quill imitates the medium olives, and you should certainly carry Blue Uprights for those with a bluish tinge, and Red Quills as an alternative spinner pattern. One of the most useful of all dry flies is the Grey Duster, which is easily seen as the light fades at dusk, and, in very small sizes, gives you something to throw when the fish are taking the tiny white flies known as the 'Angler's Curse', which hatch from late June onwards in thousands, often causing vigorous rises in the early morning. The Grey Duster in a size 8 or 10 is also a good answer to a hatch of mayfly. In my experience it is more effective than any of the special mayfly patterns, and I would happily fish the mayfly season with nothing else.

MATCHING THE HATCH

Imagine yourself on the bank of a lake early one morning in the second week in June. The water is still calm, its surface like glass, and here and there along the shore are the ebbing rings of rising trout. What should you tie on the end of your line?

Watch the fish carefully. Rises mean fish feeding high

in the water, probably on something ascending to hatch. But how high in the water? If you can see the fishes' backs breaking the surface in a quiet but definite rise, they are probably taking something stuck beneath the surface film. At this time of day the most likely thing to be hatching will be midge pupae. Midges hatch fast, so you're unlikely to see any on the water but they should be in evidence in the air around. Flies on the surface will probably be olives, and the rise may be to olive nymphs, but if there are midges in the air, best start fishing with a midge pupa. But which one? If you can catch one of the flying insects you can get some idea of the size and colour, but failing that I would begin with a red and silver one at this time of year. If that doesn't interest the fish try a green or black; and, unless the flying insects are obviously small, start with the larger sizes because it is still early in the season. If you still get no reaction while the trout continue to rise, try an olive nymph of some kind instead.

You can see from this example that the basic principle of fly-selection is the application to what is actually happening in front of you, of what you know about the trout and the fly. You are trying to match the fly in the water with the best imitation you have in your box, and if you cannot see the fly in the water you must work out what it is from the behaviour of the fish and what you know it *ought* to be at the season and time in question.

The principle can be illustrated with further examples. Later in our June day the breeze will begin, causing a ripple on the water. The rise will have stopped, and there may be little sign of hatching flies. Now the fish are deeper, and the likeliest thing to fish with will be a representation of one of the nymphs which swim about more freely in midwater than the pupae of midges and sedges. I usually begin with a Palmer Nymph, and try it in one or two sizes before changing to another nymph, but the fly to fish with is the one you believe in, and I would even say it is better to fish these conditions with a less likely fly (a midge pupa, say) than a likely one you have no confidence in.

About half past eight the breeze often falters and dies. The ripple then flattens out and the water is calm again, and these are just the sort of conditions that midges and sedges like for hatching, so the evening rise will soon begin. The problem now will be telling which fly the fish are taking, since they may feed on both at once, or become 'preoccupied' with one or the other. Sometimes you can tell by the sound they make: rises to midge pupae are slow and deliberate; to sedges, especially the adults, they tend to be more splashy, like someone slapping the water with their hand. On water where more than one fly is allowed, there is something to be said for hedging your bets. You can put a dry sedge on the point, and a hatching pupa and a midge pupa higher up the leader. The only problem is that teams of flies tangle much more easily than single ones, and with darkness coming on, tangles will be something to avoid. Perhaps the best thing is to fish intelligently, and not persevere doggedly with a fly that gets no reaction. On the other hand, remember you can only catch trout with your fly in the water, so give it a chance; changing it every third cast will only make you frustrated, and you will probably miss the fish that does take it.

On the stream, if you time your fishing right, you can arrive at the water about half an hour before you expect the rise. The trout may well be feeding, of course, even though they are not rising, but unless you are lucky enough to have fishing on gin-clear water you may not be able to see them doing it. In the absence of rises, fish a nymph in the likely places; I usually start with a Hare's Ear, changing to an Olive Nymph if there is no response, but once again, the nymph you trust is best. But there is no point in fishing 'blank' water with a dry-fly in the hopes that something will 'come up'. You stand far more chance of catching trout if you offer them what they are most likely to be feeding on.

Before the rise begins you usually get advance warning by seeing flies beginning to hatch. Olives are quite unmistakable. They look like tiny sailing boats being swept down the current; often you can catch one to see its size and colour, and this will help you in the selection of the artificial. But if feeding trout refuse your first choice, change to something else. It's you who are wrong, not them.

It is important during the rise, to spend time watching what the fish are doing; the same applies in the case of individual fish who may be rising at other times of day. Make sure a fish is taking either duns or spinners before you cast a dry-fly to it, or you may scare it needlessly. If it is taking hatching nymphs below the surface, or swimming nymphs lower down, it may not come up to a dry-fly and you may scare it with your cast, whereas a nymph passing beneath the surface, even if not taken by the fish, will cause less commotion. And once again, bear in mind the stage of the season and the time of day; evening rises, for instance, may be caused by falling spinners or sedges, as well as hatches of olives, and it is often worth starting with a Pheasant Tail if you are fishing in the evening.

Above all, remember the principles. What you are up to is deducing from what you can see, coupled with what you know about trout and flies, what fly is the most likely to appeal to the fish. You will not always be right, but at least, when you are not, you will be wrong for the right reason, and you will be right far more times than not, which will give you a great advantage over people whose fly selection is based on chucking and chancing it.

4 Presenting the Fly

Selecting the right fly is an important step in the direction of catching trout. But it is only a step, and it is not catching fish. To do that you must present the fly to the fish in such a way that it is deceived into taking it; presentation is the most important aspect of fishing.

Consider an artificial fly; compare it with the real thing. The natural is glowing, translucent, *alive:* the imitation is dull, opaque, lifeless. How can any trout, even allowing for the fact that it works by instinct rather than by reasoned thought, mistake one for the other?

The reason is not because the imitation looks so like the real thing that the trout would mistake it under any circumstances, but because it looks *sufficiently* like the real thing to deceive the trout *in the right circumstances*. If a trout is feeding on olive duns, and along comes something that sits on the water like a dun, in the overall shape and size of an olive, then, eight times out of ten, the trout will take it for another of the same kind; but only if it comes along on the current not only looking like a fly but acting like one. And this is what presentation is about – making your artificial fly behave the way real ones do. Once you have grasped this you will be well on the way to fishing success. But before you can present the fly, you must get it into the water, and to do that you must know how to assemble the tackle and how to cast the fly.

ASSEMBLING THE TACKLE

The essential equipment of the fly fisher is in five parts: first the rod, really just a long, flexible spring, capable of throwing very light weights, and of absorbing the jerks and struggles of a hooked fish; second, the reel, which is merely a winch for winding and storing the line; third, the line, which is both the weight thrown by the rod and the tether which secures the hooked fish; fourth the leader, a length of nylon between the point of the line and the fly, which helps in the deception by keeping the fly and the rather thick line apart; and fifth, the fly, which deceives the trout. Assembling this equipment is simple. You start with the line and the reel and must first decide which hand you want to wind with. Most right-handed fishermen use the left hand for winding, so as to leave the right free for controlling the rod, and this will mean the line must be wound on from the left-hand side as the spool faces you (see Figure 17). Fly lines usually come in lengths of 30 yards, more than enough for casting, but not usually enough to fill a reel, and the extra room on the spool is filled with thinner backing, fastened to the line with a splice or needle-knot (see p. 79). Any good tackle dealer will do this for you, and supply you with a

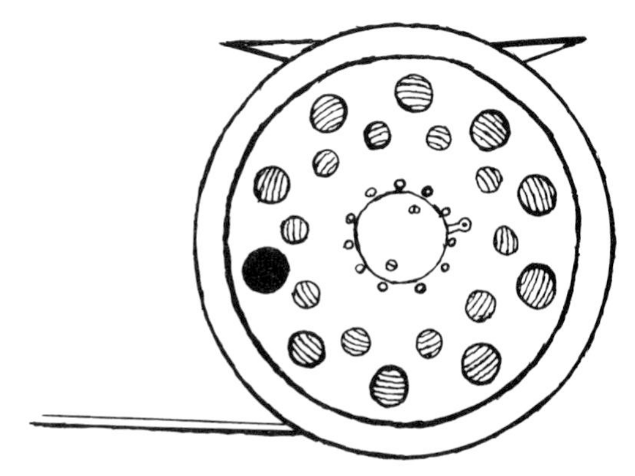

Figure 17 Reel with line fitted for left hand wind.

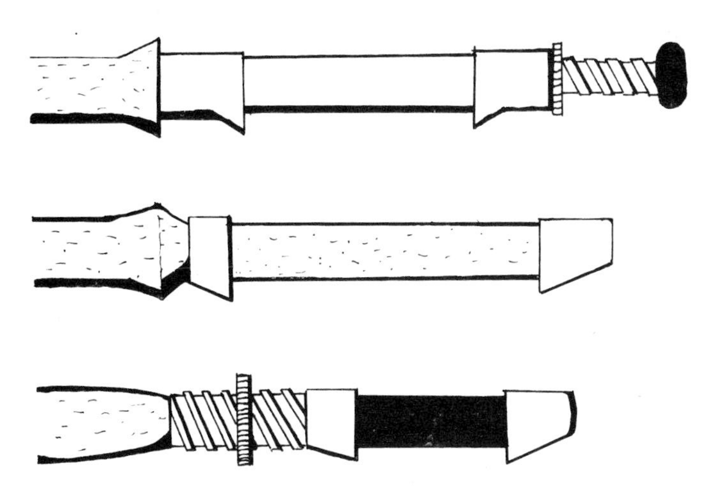

Figure 18 Some of the winch fittings available on the rods.

reel with line and backing fitted, though it is not difficult to do yourself if you want to: I never trust anyone else's knots myself.

The reel, complete with line is then fitted to the butt of the rod (Figure 18). Most fly-rods come with a screw-up winch-fitting into which the reel easily seats, but make sure the reel is fitted so that the line comes off it from the underside! Run the line through the rod-rings, making sure you miss none, and attach the leader. There are a number of ways this can be done: most versatile is to tie a length of nylon of the same thickness as the butt end of the leader to the point of the line, using a pin knot (see p. 79). If you then tie loops at the other end, and on the butt of your leader, it is a simple matter to join them together, or to change leaders (see Figure 19). The fly is then tied to the point of the leader using one of the knots recommended on pp. 79–80, and the tackle is ready for fishing.

CASTING THE FLY

Like many physical knacks, casting a fly is best learned by imitation and advice, but you may not know an

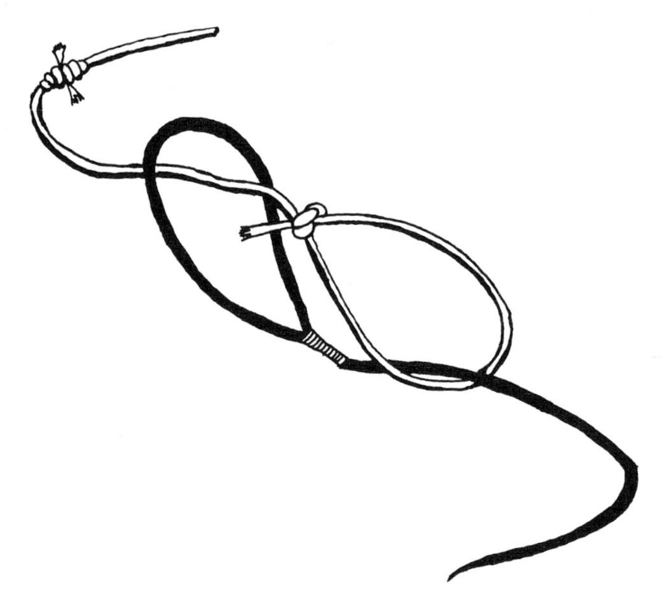

Figure 19 Line with nylon loop for cast attachment.

experienced fly-fisherman to help you, so before I start on the instructions, let me say something about the principles. Casting with a bait rod is fairly easy: you wind up the line till the weights are close to the rod-tip, then flick the rod forward, releasing the line from the reel at the critical moment so that the weights fly out in front, pulling the line behind them. The weights fly forward because the length of the rod magnifies relatively slight movement at the butt end into much more vigorous movement at the tip. This is further increased by the flexing of the rod which stores up and then releases energy which throws the weights forward. Exactly the same principles apply in the case of a fly rod, except that there are no weights: the business end of the tackle is as fine and light as possible because of our need for realistic presentation. What you cast, therefore, is the weight of the line itself, which explains why fly lines are so thick and heavy.

The standard 'vertical' cast. The angler has just begun the back-cast, by flicking the rod up and back.

The standard 'vertical' cast. The angler has just begun to forward-cast and the line is stretched out behind the rod tip.

'Shooting' line: the cast is completed and the rod has come down to the horizontal. The left hand has moved forward releasing the yard or so of line it can be seen holding in the previous photo.

But casting the weight of the line involves another difference. Where the bait-fisherman's weights are physically small and heavy, yours (the line) is long and extended, and because of this, *you can only throw it in one direction when it is already stretched out behind the rod-tip in another*. So a fly-cast involves two movements – the back-cast and the forward-cast. What you have to do is this: using the rod, throw the line up in the air behind you, and, when you feel the weight of the line beginning to pull on the rod-tip, throw it forward again. After each movement, back and forward, you pause for a moment: as you will see from Figure 20 the line at first travels through the air behind the rod-tip which is pulling it; when the rod is stopped at the end of each movement, the line continues to move, but, being anchored to the rod-tip, it does so by 'unrolling' in the air behind or in front of you, and the pause gives time for the line to finish unrolling. As it straightens on the back-cast you can feel it pulling at the rod-tip: then is the time to cast forward.

Figure 20a Rod-tip movement in the back-cast.

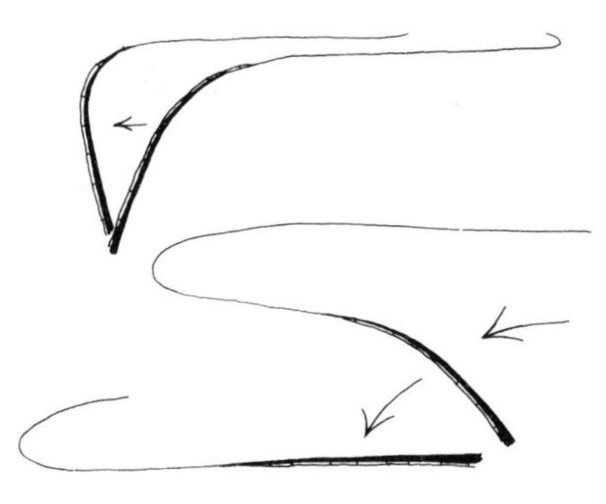

b Rod-tip movement in the forward-cast.

So much for principles, now for practice. Find an open space (preferably without too many passers-by who will only make rude remarks) if possible by a bit of water – the boating pond in the local park will do very well. Assemble the tackle and hold the rod comfortably in the right hand, much as you would a tennis or squash racquet. (If you are left-handed, you will have to read left for right and *vice versa* in this bit). Pull off about 10 feet of line through the rings (not counting the leader) and drop it in loose coils on the ground in front of you; then pull off another yard or so with the left hand between the reel and the butt ring, and hold on to it. Keeping the left

Figure 21 The back-cast.

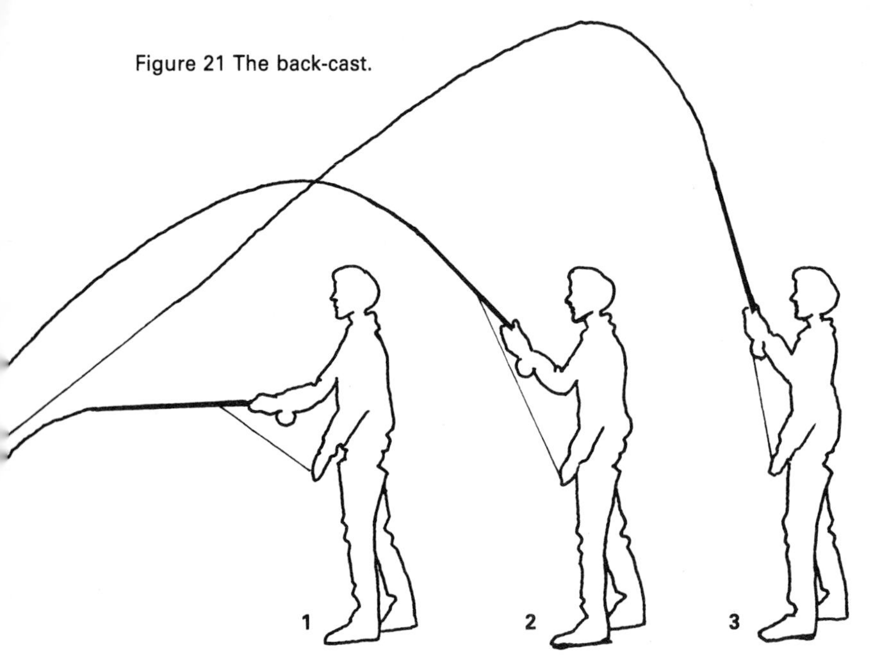

hand still, about waist height, flick the rod up in the air behind you with the right as though you were trying to throw the line vertically upwards, and pause (see Figure 21). Never, never try and throw the line straight out behind you: this will only result in your swishing the rod *too far* back, when the line, instead of flying out in the air, will pile up in a heap on the ground.

If you like you can watch the line unrolling behind you, but it is probably better to judge the moment for the forward cast by feel; when you feel the line beginning to pull on the rod, flick the rod forward again, but not too far: don't try and *drive* the line down to the water but flick it forward in the air, pause again, and flick it back again, pause, flick forward. See Figure 22. This is called false-casting, and is a very useful technique, both for measuring your cast to a rising fish, and for working out more line. If, on the forward-cast, you let go of the line in the left hand as the line in the air straightens, it will 'shoot' out through the rings, and you can then strip some more off the reel on the backcast to shoot on the next forward-

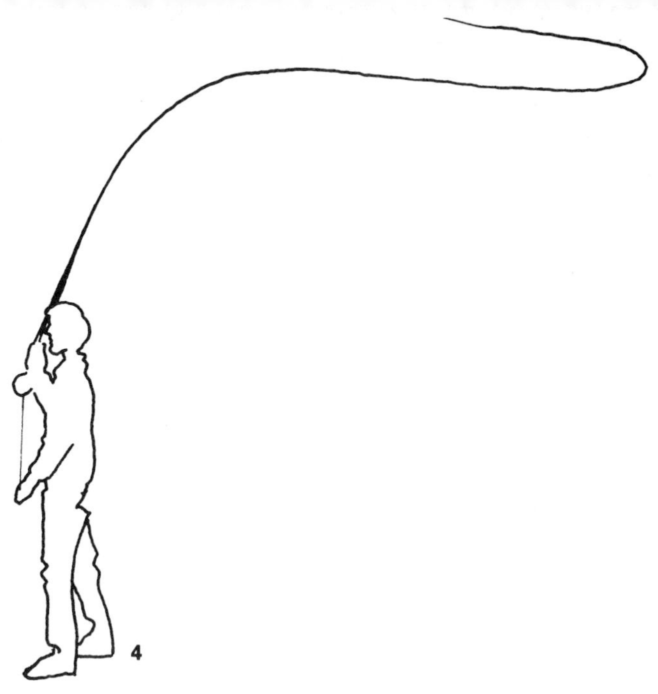

cast. Don't try and shoot too much to begin with, but always shoot some as you make the final forward-cast. This is done in precisely the same way, except that, instead of flicking the line back when it straightens, you allow it to fall to the water (or ground) in front of you, lowering the rod-tip and shooting the last bit of line as it does so.

Half an hour or so of practice will enable you to get hold of the basic technique, though it will be a long time before you win any casting competitions! But that doesn't matter. You aren't trying to break distance records, you are learning to fish, and accuracy, and above all, gentleness, are far more important than length. Casting is not an end in itself. It is simply the most effective way of getting the fly into the water quietly and without disturbance.

When you are fishing, it is always best to cast with the rod as near the horizontal as possible. You will realise from what has been said about trout vision that a vertical rod is much more likely to scare fish than one kept low.

The movements are precisely the same with the rod horizontal, except that they are on their side, as it were; you can, of course, cast in any plane. You will often find it necessary to vary the plane of the cast in this way because of bankside obstructions like trees and bushes. You can also cast backhanded over the left shoulder, and as you get more practised you will find that you can begin changing direction between back and forward casts, so that, on a lake, for instance, you can move from a rising fish directly in front of you to one at the side with a false cast or two. But don't try to change direction too

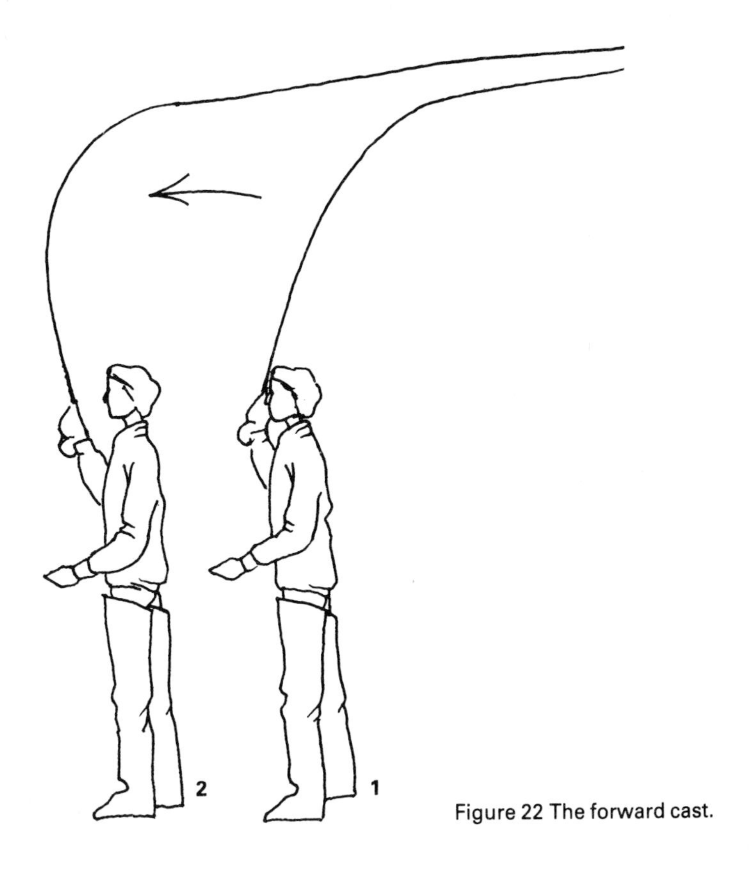

Figure 22 The forward cast.

far at once to begin with, or you may wrap the fly round your neck.

JUDGING THE DEPTH

However well you cast and present your fly, it won't achieve much unless it is where the fish are. When they are obviously rising steadily at the surface there are few problems: all you have to do is present your fly among the naturals the fish are taking, so you treat it with

Horizontal cast: the angler is starting the back-cast. Note how the rod is kept flat.

Horizontal cast: the angler has just completed the back-cast and is pausing while the line unrolls behind the rod tip.

floatant (see p. 80) to sit on the surface without sinking. Many dry-fly fishermen also grease their leader down to the point so that it will not sink and drag the fly under, but tests have shown that a greased leader on the surface is much more obvious to the fish than a sunken one, and so more likely to scare them. It is better to grease only the top part of the leader, and to treat the last two or three feet at the point with something to remove grease and make the nylon cut through the surface (see p. 80).

The problems begin when fish are feeding elsewhere than the surface. If they are rising to nymphs or pupae stuck beneath it, or insects ascending to hatch, the depth at which to present your fly will be fairly obvious from the way they rise. Insects high in the water will be imitated with unweighted flies that will sink only slowly; the depth to which they sink can be controlled by greasing the leader – the more you grease the higher the fly will swim in the water. Again, however, the point should be treated with de-greaser to make it sink.

To de-grease the point of the leader, however, does not mean the fly will fish at a depth equal to the de-greased point. An unleaded fly will, in fact, gradually sink lower in the water once it is cast, but, as Figure 23 makes clear, the leader will never hang straight down: it will always lie in a gentle curve from the surface, so a fly with three feet of de-greased leader will not have sunk more than about a foot by the time the cast is fished out. And it is possible to counteract the sinking of the fly by forms of 'retrieving' (see p. 60) which will cause it to swim upwards in the water.

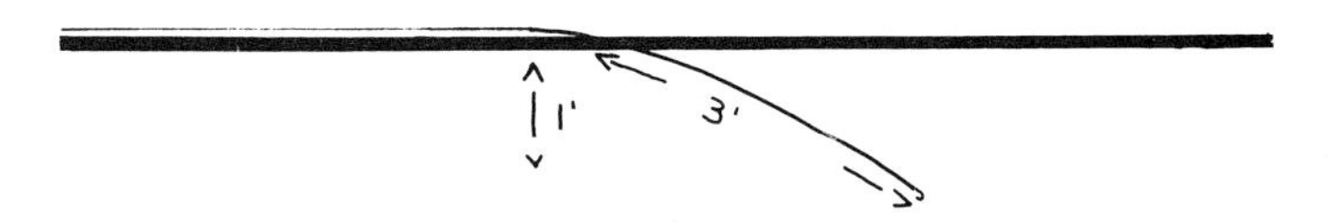

Figure 23 Although 3 feet of the leader have been left ungreased to sink at the point, the fly only fishes at a depth of a foot because the point does not hang vertically downwards in the water.

But suppose no rises are visible at the surface? In this case the fish are obviously feeding somewhere else, from midwater down, and you will have to judge how deep to fish. Various clues may help. On bright, hot days, and early in the season, you can expect trout to be fairly deep. When the stream is in spate and the water is coloured, they will be near the bottom, for shelter and for the worms swept down by the flood. In these situations you will need weighted nymphs to take the fly down to the fish, and on lakes you will need long leaders – up to 15 or 20 feet – with only a short section greased to float at the butt. And you will need to wait for the fly to sink to the depth at which you want to fish it: even a weighted nymph can take two or three minutes to get really deep, and there is no point in trying to fish it too soon.

In the absence of clues from the weather, or the time of the season, you will have to rely on trial and error. Start deep, and gradually fish higher, remembering to give the fly time to sink, and trying a variety of patterns at each depth, before fishing the higher water. On the stream, of course, you may not be able to get the fly very deep any way; the current will bring it back to you before it has had time to sink very far, and it will go deepest where the current is slowest. Weighted patterns are often necessary on streams even for fish you can see feeding, because unweighted ones may not have time to sink more than an inch or two where the current is strong.

UPSTREAM OR DOWN?

On the lake you can cast in any direction, but on the stream you are faced with a choice between casting so that the current brings the fly back towards you (upstream, including up-and-across-the-stream), or casting so that it takes it away (downstream, including down-and-across). With the dry fly you always have to cast upstream to avoid the problem of 'drag' (p. 61), but with the nymph you must decide, when you begin to fish whether to move and cast upstream or down. On some

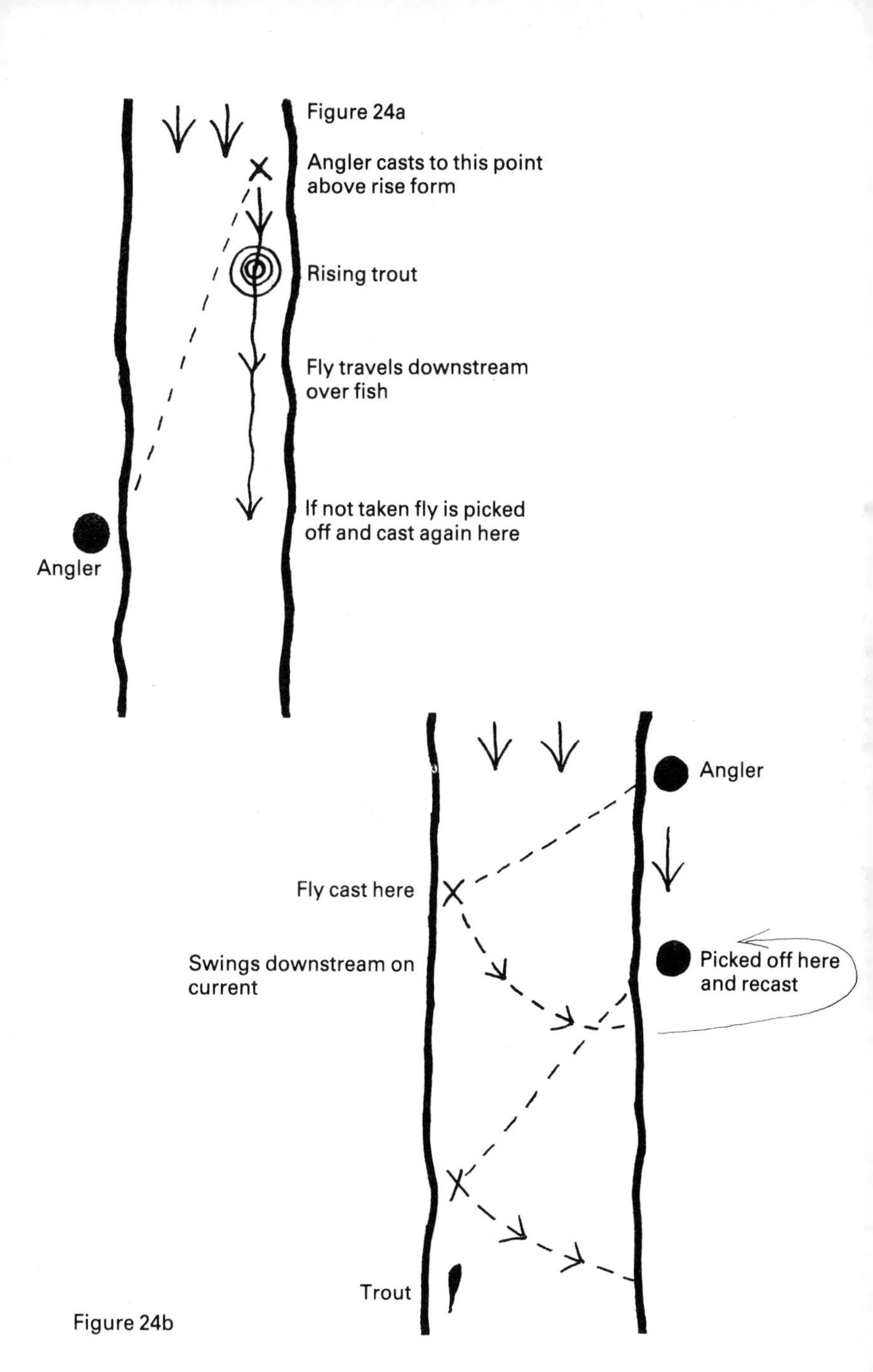
Figure 24a
Angler casts to this point above rise form
Rising trout
Fly travels downstream over fish
If not taken fly is picked off and cast again here
Angler
Angler
Fly cast here
Swings downstream on current
Picked off here and recast
Trout
Figure 24b

streams the decision is out of your hands: the rules permit only upstream casting.

Upstream fishing is more rewarding, but it has the reputation of being the most difficult fly-fishing method. It is also a deadly way of fishing for trout. You must grease the leader to float, apart from the point, and cast the fly on a fairly short line upstream, or up-and-across, so as to enter the water a yard or two above where you believe the fish to be. The current will carry the fly down, sinking as it goes, over the place where the fish lies, and back towards you, and as it does so you must retrieve the line through the rod-rings with your left hand (most easily done if you trap the line against the rod-butt with your right forefinger at the same time). If you don't, the current will take over, catching the line beneath the rod-tip, and dragging it out into a long belly behind you, and when the fish takes the fly you will be totally unable to tighten on it and set the hook. Takes will be revealed by the point of the leader, where it enters the water: when the fish seizes the fly the leader will twitch, stab down, or draw smoothly away, and when it does so you must strike like lightning – by then the fish is already beginning to spit out the fly! If you don't get a take first time, try several times more before moving on or changing the fly, especially if the fish keeps feeding: the fact that it doesn't select your nymph the first time need not mean it has refused it.

Downstream nymph-fishing is a technique for high water early in the season, or for casting to a fish that cannot be reached from below. A weighted fly is cast down and across the stream, at an angle of some 45 degrees, and allowed to swing round on the current until it is under your own bank. Then you must take a pace or two downstream and cast again. Takes will be felt as a tug at the end of the line, and you should tighten more deliberately than with the upstream nymph, for you may pull the fly out of the fish's mouth if you are too quick. Try and fish the fly round as slowly as possible, but don't hold it against the flow of the current: natural nymphs can make little headway against the full force of the stream, and the fish will suspect one that breasts the current like a cross-channel swimmer! You can present the downstream nymph lower in the water by using a sinking line, and you should, in any case, treat the whole leader to sink, and use a weighted nymph. But if you can see trout on the feed I would fish upstream to them – it's much deadlier.

IMPARTING 'LIFE'

The greatest difference of all between natural and artificial flies is that natural flies are alive. One of your main objectives, therefore, must be to give the appearance of life when presenting your fly to the fish. There is only one way of doing this: life, for our purposes, means movement, and we must therefore make our flies move. Some flies are dressed in such a way as to give the appearance of movement, for instance the Palmer nymph (see Figure 13, p.37) whose hackles reflect the light and give the appearance of a 'fuzz' of movement. But whether the fly is dressed this way or not, it must move, and the movement must be supplied by the fisherman.

This is particularly important on lakes, where there is no current. In the stream the current moves the fly and helps create the impression of life (though you can aid the deception too). In any case, tiny nymphs and flies can make little headway against the current, and most of their movements are made with it, so there is not the same need for the angler to concentrate on moving the fly. But on the lake there is only one way to impart 'life': by pulling on the line.

Retrieving, then, is an essential part of lake fishing. The fly is cast and then retrieved, either by left-hand pulls on the line, or by raising the rod tip and gathering in the slack line. Raising the rod will move the fly relatively quickly, and for several feet – so much so that it will probably lift in the water. When the rod is then lowered and the slack gathered by the left hand, the fly

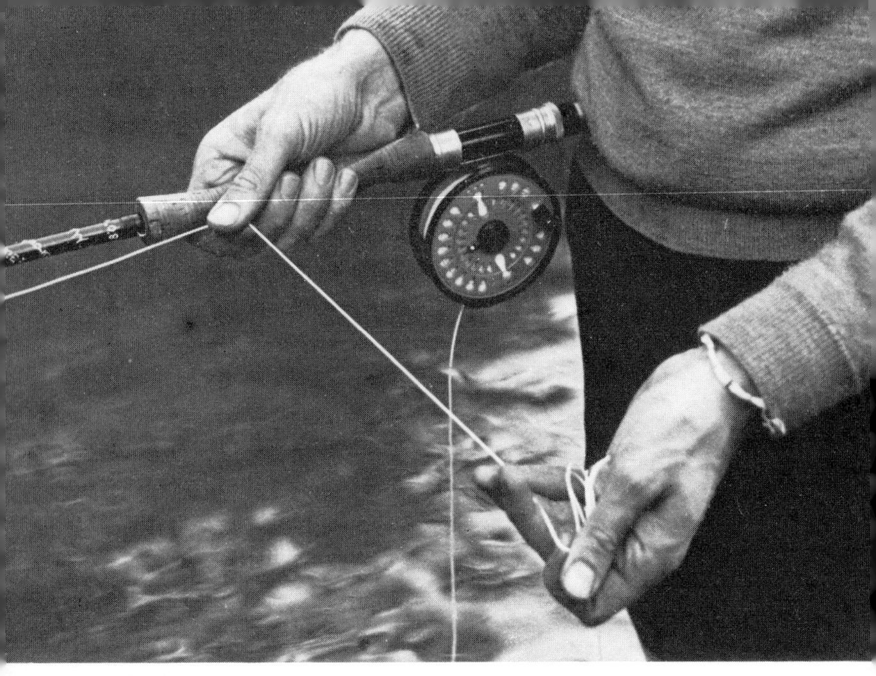

Angler retrieving the line while fishing upstream. The method is the same for dry fly, upstream nymph and lake fishing. Note how the left hand draws the line through the thumb and forefinger of the right hand.

will sink again, and this 'sink-and-draw' method is particularly good for imitating insects ascending to hatch. Pulling with the left hand moves the fly less far at a time, and flatter in the water, like nymphs swimming in midwater, or insects stuck beneath the surface. Either method can be quick or slow, and you must vary the speed to suit the insect you are imitating; and remember, real insects do not move in steady six-inch jerks, with half a second's pause between. Fish imaginatively, picturing to yourself what the fly is doing as you retrieve, and trying to make it behave as the real insect would.

Sink-and-draw has an application to the stream. If you know a fish is taking nymphs in a certain place you can often encourage it to take yours by casting well upstream so that the fly has time to sink below the level of the trout by the time it reaches it. Then, as the nymph swims down towards the fish, a sudden lift of the rod-tip will make the fly lift in the water, and can be judged for that moment when the fly is just in front of the fish. More often than not such a lifting of the nymph will result in an immediate take by the fish.

DEALING WITH DRAG

There are, of course, times when you won't want to move the fly. These will be mainly when stream fishing with the dry fly. Duns and spinners remain fairly still on the surface, drying their wings or laying their eggs, and your aim in presenting their imitations must be to allow them to drift naturally on the current. The problem here is that the fly is attached to the line, and when you have cast it, not just the fly, but the line as well will be drifting on the current, and very likely the line will be lying across the current too. But streams do not flow at the same speed across their width; the water in the middle moves quicker, and there are back eddies, obstructions and so on (see Figure 25). So the water where the fish is,

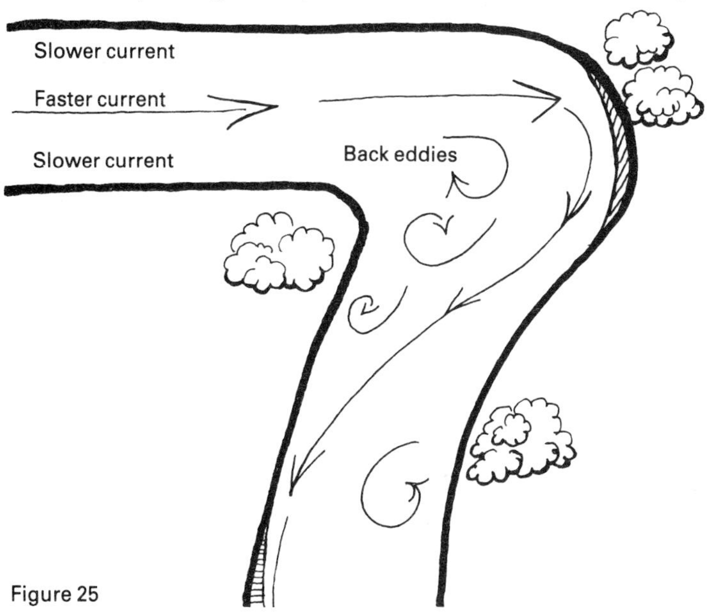

Figure 25

and where the fly lands, may be moving slower or faster than the water between you and it, where the line is.

Figure 26 makes clear what happens. The faster water will pull the line into a belly which then acts on the leader and fly, dragging the fly across the surface faster than the water is moving, or holding the fly against the current. In either case, a wake is created by the dragging fly, and the trout, who knows perfectly well that real flies do not drag, goes elsewhere for its dinner.

There is no way of avoiding drag altogether. The best you can do is to delay it by casting a waggle in the line, (Figure 27a) or by flicking a loop of line upstream once the fly has alighted and before it gets anywhere near the trout. Casting a waggle will be no problem to you as a beginner. The difficulty will be getting it straight, but you can do it on purpose by giving the rod a shake as you shoot the last few feet of line. This will put the line on the

Figure 26

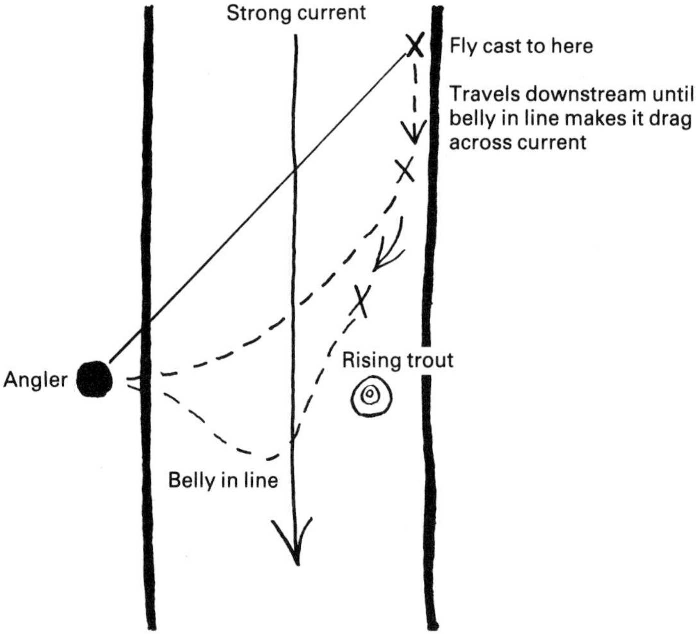

water in a series of curves which the faster current will have to straighten before it can drag the fly on the slower water. Flicking a loop of line upstream, or 'mending' the line, is also quite easy: once the line has alighted on the surface, simply flick the rod-tip in a half circle and the line will follow (Figure 27b).

Another kind of drag occurs on lakes and streams when fishing the nymph. This is drag from the leader, at the point where it enters the water, and is caused by retrieving too vigorously. Its effect on the fly is not very

Figure 27a Casting a waggle.

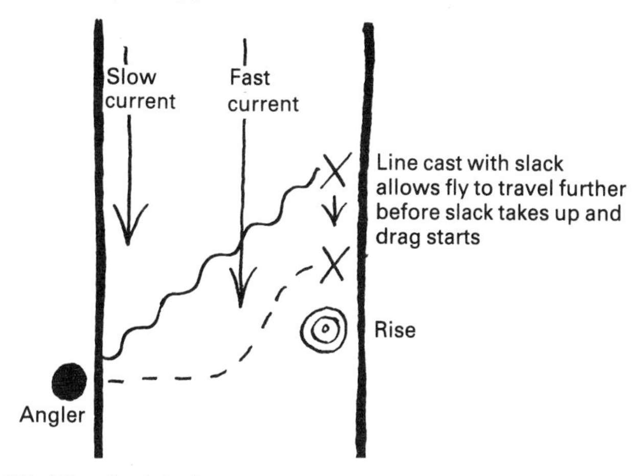

Figure 27b 'Mending' the line.

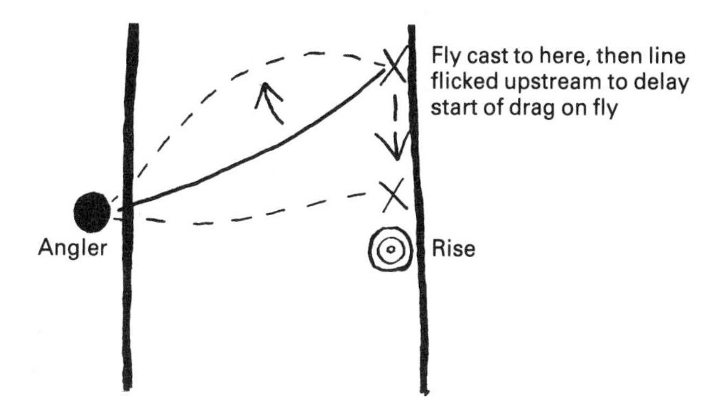

damaging to presentation, but it causes ripples of light, reflected from the wake of the leader at the surface, to pass over the bottom, and this can quickly alarm the fish. The calmer the surface the more this kind of drag is a problem, and in glassy conditions you must slow the retrieve right down so that no ripples are caused at the surface at all. This, of course means that you cannot vary the retrieve so much. On the other hand, in such conditions it is very much easier to spot the take than when the leader is obscured by ripples or waves created by the wind.

The only time when drag is a help is when you are fishing dry sedges. The natural fly scutters about the surface, causing quite a commotion, and you may well actually attract a fish to your artificial by giving it the occasional tweak on the surface, creating a wake, and causing a disturbance. Mind you, I have caught my share of trout on dragging dry flies, and so has many another – but that's another story.

5 Catching the Trout

Suppose you have arrived at the water, interpreted the behaviour of the fish, identified the fly and matched it and presented it in a lifelike way: how do you know when the fish has taken your fly, and what do you do when it does?

SPOTTING THE TAKE

With a dry fly, spotting the take is easy. You simply watch the fly coming down the current towards you, and when the fish rises to it you see the whole thing. The water heaves, a dark snout appears and the fly vanishes in the centre of the rise. But if you are fishing nymphs things are more complicated. When you are presenting the fly downstream, you may well see the whole line twitch, and you will certainly feel the tug of the trout taking the fly, though you will often fail to hook it. But in upstream and lake fishing, where there is no current keeping the line taut between rod-tip and fly, you may see very little, and if you wait until you feel the pull of the fish you will almost certainly catch nothing. Nevertheless, the signs of the take will be there if you have eyes to see them.

If the fish is high in the water you may see a bulge or hump in the surface near the end of the leader, but the basic sign of a take is the delicate movement of the leader on the surface as the fly is taken into the fish's mouth. This movement may vary from the distinct and definite to something almost imperceptible, depending on a series of factors. Like the humping of water at the surface, it results from the fact that the fish can only seize the fly by a movement of its whole body: the slower your retrieve, therefore, the slower the fish will have to move to seize the fly, and the more delicate the take will be. The classic sign of a fish taking an upstream or stillwater nymph is a sliding of the leader through the 'hole' in the surface where the ungreased point dips down into the water; it may be a slow draw, a sudden stab, a jerk or a tiny twitch. The leader may move an inch or a foot or more, and it may move sideways or even, in some cases, appear to get longer, if the fish is intercepting the fly from your side of it and lifting the leader in the water. And it may be that the leader will not move at all; the experienced nymph fisherman can often give no reason for why he struck a particular fish: he develops a 'sixth sense' which detects minute alterations in the arrangement of the leader and the surface around it which transmits the message 'take' to the brain without any conscious process of weighing the evidence up.

Clearly the lesson of all this is the need for concentration. If you are fishing upstream – or stillwater – nymph you cannot afford to enjoy the scenery: your attention must be focussed on the leader from the moment the fly alights on the water. This, in turn, means there is no point in casting so far that you can't see the leader. In heavy ripple or waves, of course, seeing the leader is more difficult anyway, and it is quite helpful to tie on a dry sedge at the top of the degreased point section: this will act like a float, disappearing beneath the surface when the fly is taken, and alerting you to the take. In calm water, however, it will cause problems of drag, which may discourage the fish.

THE STRIKE

Trout do not wait to be caught. Once they have taken the fly they feel its hardness and spit it out. Occasionally the hook will set itself in the fish's jaw in the process, but normally it must be driven in by the fisherman before the fish has time to get rid of it, and this is the purpose of the strike.

Striking is simply tightening the line between the rod and the hook to drive home the hook, and the question is how hard to do it. The answer is as hard as is necessary! If the line is straight without slack to the fish, as in downstream fishing, then you will need to do no more than lift the rod-tip to tighten the line. Wrenching on the rod really hard in these circumstances might even break the leader. If there is slack in the line, however, as there often is when fishing upstream, or when the wind puts a belly in it on the surface of a lake, you must strike harder to take up the slack. You can make the strike much more effective in these conditions by pulling in line with the left hand as you raise the rod with the right. This can almost double the speed of the strike, and many fishermen do it automatically: the action is similar to the start of a casting sequence.

A secondary question about striking is how soon. With upstream or lake nymph, you cannot be too quick: by the time you see the take, the fish is already feeling the hook, and you must hit it the instant the take is seen. In downstream fishing you can afford to take a little longer. There is a danger that too quick a strike will whip the fly out of the fish's mouth before it turns across the stream, especially as the line will be fairly taut already. Slowest of all is the strike with the dry fly, when you must wait until the fish has turned down with the fly before tightening. Fish rising to dry flies (see Figure 28) may come up beneath them or turn out of the water on to them, but in either case, if you strike as the fish breaks the surface, you will be snatching the fly away before it has proper hold of it. Striking to the dry fly calls for self control: you have to force yourself *not* to strike too soon, and if you find you are missing rises to your fly, the chances are you need to slow the strike down, not speed it up. I once missed seventeen fish on a Cornish reser-

Figure 28 Trout rise – when to strike on a dry fly.

voir, fishing with a dry sedge, through striking too soon!

PLAYING THE FISH

When you drive the hook in, the fish's initial reaction will probably be a brief pause to assess the situation, followed by a determined effort to escape. Occasionally the prick of the hook will cause a fish to bolt, especially if the take itself was hard and the fish hooked itself; a hard strike then can easily result in a smashed leader, and in any case the harder you hold a fish the more likely it will be to try and run for it. But there is no virtue in prolonging the fight unnecessarily: playing a fish causes it distress, and it is plain cruelty to do it for longer than necessary. So play your fish as hard as your tackle will stand, and get the fight over as soon as you can.

The trout's basic instinct when hooked is to seek shelter, so you can expect it to dive for weed, underwater roots and other hideouts. If it is a rainbow trout, it may very well attempt to shake the hook out by splashing or leaping clear of the water, but brown trout tend to go deep and fight with a dour shaking of the head. Any of these can cause you problems. Weeds and underwater obstructions can foul and break the line, splashing at the surface quickly weakens the hook hold, and the brow-

Angler playing a fish. Note how the tip of the rod bends while the rod is kept relatively upright. The bend 'cushions' the fine point against sudden pulls by the trout.

nie's head-down struggles can straighten the hook if it is a sizeable fish. And holding the fish too hard may tear out the hook or break the leader. So playing the fish is a matter of balancing these factors against each other.

What you have to try and do is to keep the fish under control while steering it with the rod away from likely obstructions, and the key to the process is the rod itself. The bending of the rod acts as a cushion against the pulls of the fish, absorbing the effects of its struggles, and so protecting the fine point of the leader from snapping. You must therefore keep the rod butt upright so that the rod can flex fully. If you once let the fish pull on the line directly from the reel without the cushioning curve of the rod you can say goodbye to it. When the rod is well bent, of course, there is less margin of safety, so a strong pull from the fish will mean you need to let it take line off the reel.

Steering the fish is best done by using side-strain –

Angler applying side strain with the rod to steer a fish away from a weed bed.

lowering the rod to a horizontal position while keeping the same angle between the butt and the fish. If it is determined to go to weed or some other obstruction, there may be no alternative but to hold it hard and risk a break, but even if it does gain the sanctuary of a weed bed, you can sometimes keep in touch by letting everything go slack, and waiting until it moves out again before putting the pressure on once more. The other thing to avoid is letting a fish splash at the surface. Apart from the fact that it will disturb other fish in the vicinity, it can loosen the hook very quickly, so if the fish comes to the surface, slacken your hold, and it will go down again. If it leaps, drop the rod tip, in case it lands on the tight leader and snaps it, but tighten up again once it is back in the water.

Your aim in playing the fish is to keep it under control while gradually shortening the line and tiring the fish to the point where it will lie still at the surface (on its side) and you can net it. Shortening the line can be done by reeling in or by stripping the line by hand; the traditional method is to play the fish 'off the reel' which avoids loops of line lying about the bank and snagging round your feet or vegetation if the fish runs and needs to take some line out. On the other hand, if you are fishing upstream or on a lake, the chances are you will already have some line in hand when the fish takes, and to play it off the reel you will have to wind this up first, so some fishermen prefer to play the fish 'from the hand', without using the reel unless the fish takes out all the slack line in the fight. On a lake you can sometimes compromise: where there is plenty of sea-room you can hold the fish hard to make it run and take out the slack, while moving backwards up the bank yourself; but on the stream you will have to hold the fish by trapping the line with the right hand while winding it up with the left, and this can be the most dangerous moment of all. I prefer to play off the reel when I can – but you must find the style that suits you best.

LANDING THE FISH

If all goes well the fish will eventually come up to the surface and lie exhausted on its side. Then and only then is the time to net it. If you attempt to net it too soon you will frighten it with the net, and it may easily gain leverage on the net frame with its tail to break the leader. So don't unship the net from its ring until the fish is lying docile in the upper water; you can tell the moment by lifting the trout's head with the line: if you can lift its head clear of the water without stimulating another run it is ready to net.

Sink the open net deeply in the water in front of you

Trout played out and ready to be netted. Note how the fish is lying on the side in the surface of the water. Note too how the net has been well sunken in the water before the fish is drawn over it.

and gently draw the fish over it. Then lift net and fish together out of the water. Don't attempt to scoop the fish with the net, and move gently and deliberately, or you will panic the fish into more struggles. *Only when the fish is in the net is it caught* – and even then it may get away again if you're not careful how you handle it. If the fish is

The trout successfully netted!

obviously undersized, don't attempt to net it at all. Just slide your fingers down the leader to the fly and give it a shake, without touching the fish. The fly should come free and the fish can swim away. If you do have to hold the fish, wet your hand first. If you're not sure about the size, measure it before you either kill it or remove the

The author with a splendid 2½ lb brown trout from a small lake fishery in East Anglia.

hook, and even if you know you are going to kill it, do so before you take the hook out so as to spare the fish unnecessary suffering. The best way to kill a fish is to knock it smartly on the head two or three times – you can get an instrument called a 'priest' (for administering the last rites!) for the purpose. If you have to handle a fish before releasing it, hold it for a moment or two upright in the water, facing upstream before allowing it to swim away.

It may seem strange in a book on fishing, to speak about sparing the fish unnecessary cruelty. In my view (which I recognise not all anglers share) the only justification for going fishing is that the fish I catch are eaten, either by myself or friends. I believe, therefore, that you ought to stop fishing when you have caught and killed your limit, and I can see no justification for fishing for the sake of it and putting all the fish back. Some people think that is less cruel than killing fish to eat, but to me it seems more cruel and quite unjustifiable to use living creatures as playthings in that way. Whatever view you take on this issue, however, (and it is going to become a bigger issue in the future) I hope you will never inflict unnecessary suffering on any fish, either thoughtlessly or on purpose. Angling has traditionally been known as 'the gentle art' and I, for one, hope it stays that way.

6 Fly Fishing Tackle

The opening of so many day-ticket fisheries has resulted in a dramatic increase in the number of fly-fishers. This has made fly fishing tackle big business, and choosing it can be a confusing experience. The aim of this chapter is to give you an idea of the basic essentials.

RODS

The rod will probably be the most expensive single item, but it need not be *too* expensive – it is best to start with something cheap and serviceable until your fishing tastes become established. If your fishing will be mainly on the larger lakes you will need a rod capable of throwing a long line delicately, without exhausting your arm in a full day's fishing. If you will be fishing small lakes or streams your main interest will be accuracy, but you must bear in mind the size of the water and the amount of vegetation on the banks. Fishing with a long rod in dense undergrowth is not much fun.

For lake use buy a rod of about 9 feet with a fairly easy action, and not too heavy. The 'action' of the rod is how it feels in the hand *with the reel and line fitted.* A stiff-actioned rod will bend most between the middle and the tip, and will feel more powerful, but requires more effort in use. An easy action means a rod that flexes most between middle and butt and feels less powerful in the hand: it will not cast so long a line but is more accurate and gives greater delicacy in presentation. You can get some idea of what a rod will be like by checking the size of line it is meant to throw. Every rod has an optimum size of line, usually marked on the butt, and for rods of a given length, the higher the line-number, the stiffer the action. A 9-foot No. 6 rod should be about right for the newcomer to lake fishing.

For the stream you will need something a little shorter, and if you fish brooks you may need one as short as 7½ feet, though that is a bit short for a beginner. Look for something between 8 and 8¾ feet with a medium to easy action. That does not mean the rod should feel soft and sloppy in the hand: it should be crisp and positive, and a rod of this length designed to throw a No. 5 or 6 line should be about right.

Three kinds of fly rod are available today: carbon-fibre, cane and glass-fibre. Carbon is the most expensive and I would not recommend it for a beginner as the advantages do not outweigh the greater cost. Cane is the traditional material of the river. It is delightful to handle, but much heavier than carbon or glass, and, therefore, really unsuited to lake use. I would recommend that you start with a glass rod since glass-fibre is light, very strong and reasonably priced.

FLY LINES

The choice of the rod determines the size of the line, but you will find that lines are made in a variety of shapes, and either to sink or to float. For the kind of fishing I have been writing about you need a floating line; the only time I would recommend a sinking one is for down-stream nymph fishing in heavy water. Get your line in a double-taper shape. That means the belly of the line is thick, tapering at each end. A tapered line is the best for delicate presentation, and when one end of a double-taper is worn you can turn the line round on the reel and fish with the other. As to colour, tests have shown that green is least visible to the fish for most of the time.

REELS AND BACKING

Don't spend a lot of money on an expensive reel – save it for day-tickets! All the reel needs to do is to hold the line without tangling it and wind it up when required, and the simpler the better. For lake fishing you want one with room for plenty of backing, just in case you hook a monster, but on the stream a smaller one will do just as well. The main thing is to get the weight right. When the reel is fitted to the rod, loaded with the line, you should not be specially aware of the weight of the reel, and the point of balance of the tackle should be somewhere in the top inch of the cork handle. If the reel is too light the rod will feel longer and heavier. If it is too heavy you will be conscious of its weight when casting. Make sure the one you buy is reversible for left-hand winding, and avoid anything with gears, multipliers or clockwork mechanisms.

THE LEADER

For delicate presentation you will need tapered leaders, which you can buy or make. Bought ones have no knots, and are expensive. Home-made ones are perfectly effective. For stream fishing they need to be fairly short – about a foot less than the length of the rod is ideal – for the sake of accuracy. On the lake you may need leaders up to 20 feet, and you should normally fish with one of 12, but length is not the only consideration: you must also decide how thick (and therefore how strong) you want the point to be. The size of the point is related to the size of the fly and the fish, and on the stream a point of 2½lb breaking-strain is usually about right. (Breaking strain relates to deadweight in air, and fish weigh rather less in water, so you can handle fish up to 3 or 4lbs on a point of that size). In lakes, leader points of 4 or 5lbs are preferable, since you will often be using rather bigger flies, and in some cases fishery owners recommend even larger nylon, but this takes account of lure fishing in which smash-takes are more common; such heavy leaders would make presentation of the nymph practically impossible.

Figure 29 shows the various knots used in making a leader and attaching it to the fly and the line. If you first pin-knot a short length of nylon to the line with a loop at the free end, you can form a loop on the butt of the leader and connect them. But the butt of the leader should be about 25lbs b-s., and about ⅓ the total length. The point should be at least 18 inches long, and the rest made of about 6 equal sections of decreasing thickness – say 15, 12, 9, 7, 5 and 4lbs b-s. The sections are joined with blood knots and the point attached to the fly with a tucked half-blood or a double turl knot. Remember that every time you change a fly, or snap the point in a bush, the leader gets shorter, so you will need to carry a spool of the same size nylon as the point for making replacements while fishing.

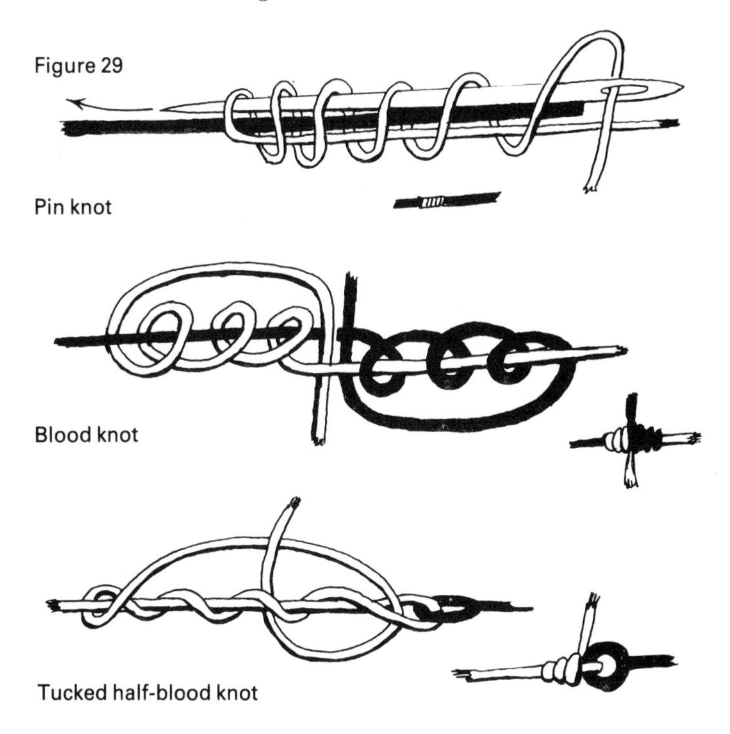

Figure 29

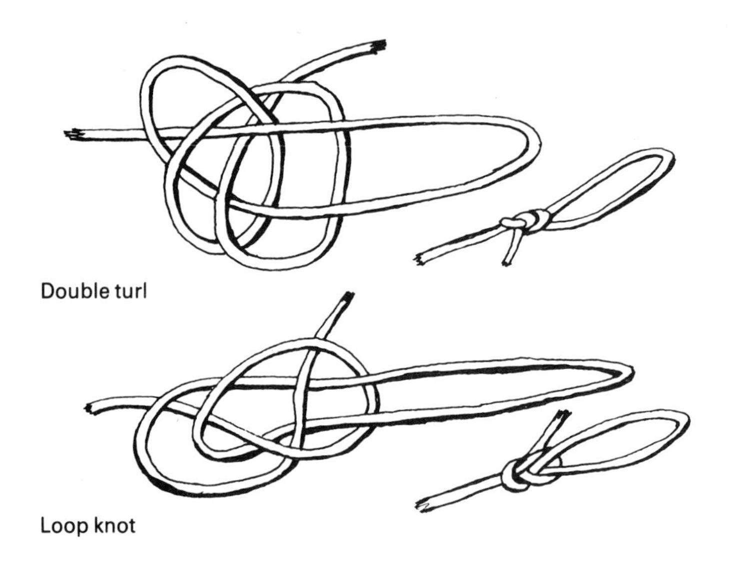
Double turl

Loop knot

SUNDRIES

You will need a bag to hold things: an old army haversack will do very well. Keep a plastic bin-liner in it to hold the fish you catch. You will also need a pair of straight nail scissors, with one blade filed to a point for poking out the eyes of flies that are blocked with varnish or old knots, and you can attach the scissors to the bag with a long rubber band. You will need line grease and degreaser, and fly-floatant. Degreaser you can make from a paste of fuller's earth powder and washing-up liquid; the others you can buy, and if you are fishing streams it is worthwhile treating all your flies regularly with a long-term floatant, as well as carrying a small aerosol floatant for touching them up while fishing. You will also need a priest and a fly-box, and two useful extras are a small torch and a scoop for extracting the stomach contents of fish you catch to see what they have been feeding on.

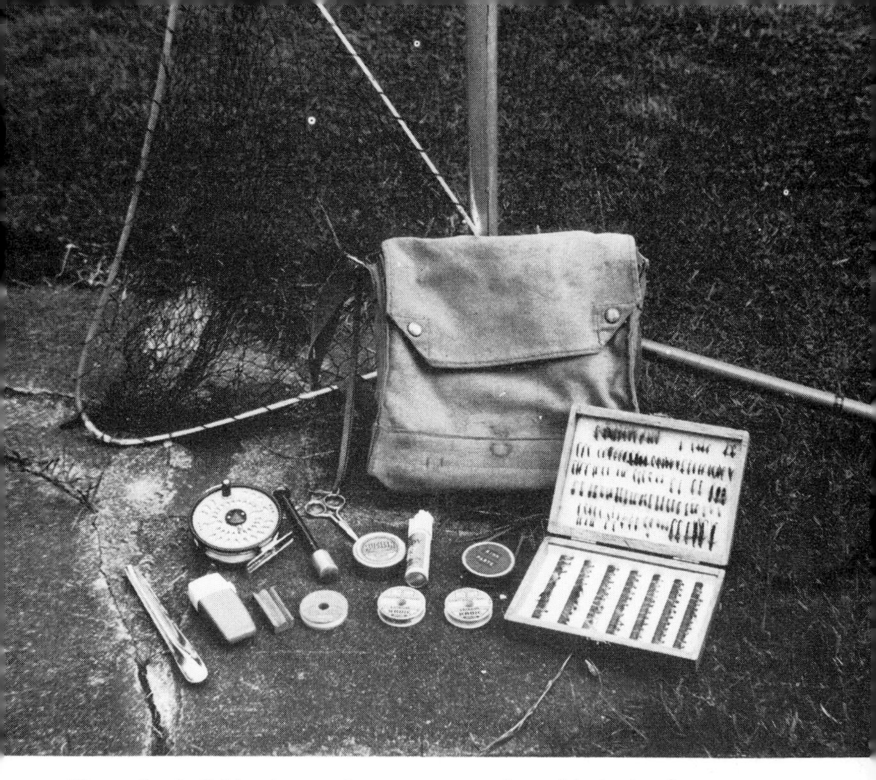

The author's fishing bag and contents, together with the landing net. The contents of the bag are as follows: background left to right: reel, 'priest', scissors (attached to bag by rubber band); line grease, fly floatant, de-greaser, fly box. Foreground, left to right: stomach 'spoon', torch, stone for sharpening hooks, nylon for repairing leader points (one spool holds white wool for dressing the breathing tubes of midge pupae).

LANDING NETS

It is unwise to go fishing without a net, but the difficulty is to know what sort to use. If you are wading a clip-on short handled net may be adequate, but where the banks are high and the water deep you will need a net with a long handle to land the fish safely. On the other hand, if you move about while fishing, a long handled net can be a great nuisance, and is easily left lying about. Perhaps best of all are clip-on folding nets with extending handles. One kind is spring-loaded so that it can be extended with one hand just when you need it. Whatever net you

A nice brace of freshly caught trout.

buy, make sure the frame is wide when opened, or you will find fish getting a purchase on it with their tails and breaking you at the critical moment.

CLOTHING

The most obvious essential is a good pair of waders. If your fishing is to be entirely in waters where the bottom is silty or muddy, as in lowland lakes and streams, you can afford to get waders with rubber soles, but for fishing in rough streams where the bottom is rocky, and in mountain lakes, nailed soles will be essential, and may even prevent a serious accident. Keep your waders in a cool place at home and away from barbed wire when fishing and they will give several years service.

Other clothing is much more a matter of personal choice. A hat with a peak is useful to shade the eyes and reduce the pale area of the face, and clothing should be chosen in accordance with the remarks about camouflage on p. 15. The main thing to remember is to avoid bright colours, and especially white.

7 Simple Fly Dressing

Nothing in fishing is so rewarding as catching a trout with a fly you made yourself. When you do so you know that *you* – and no-one else – was responsible for deceiving that fish; and once you have started fishing you will soon see all sorts of advantages in dressing your own flies.

EQUIPMENT

Start with a beginner's outfit, containing a selection of materials and basic tools. It probably won't include a vice; the best kind is one with collett-type jaws (see photograph on p. 84) and an adjustable stem. Besides a vice you will need a bobbin holder, hackle pliers, sharp curved nail scissors and a dubbing needle (see photo again). You will also need reels of tying silk in various colours, fly-tying wax and varnish, and a supply of hooks in sizes 10–16. Hooks with turned up eyes are used for dry flies, those with turned down eyes for wet flies and nymphs.

LAYING-ON AND WHIP-FINISHING

Set a size 12 hook in the vice with the point protected by the jaws, as in photograph No. 1 on p. 85, with the eye pointing to your right. Fit a spool of silk to the bobbin holder and pull off about 18 inches. Break a little wax from the lump and mould it into a ball, then pull the silk

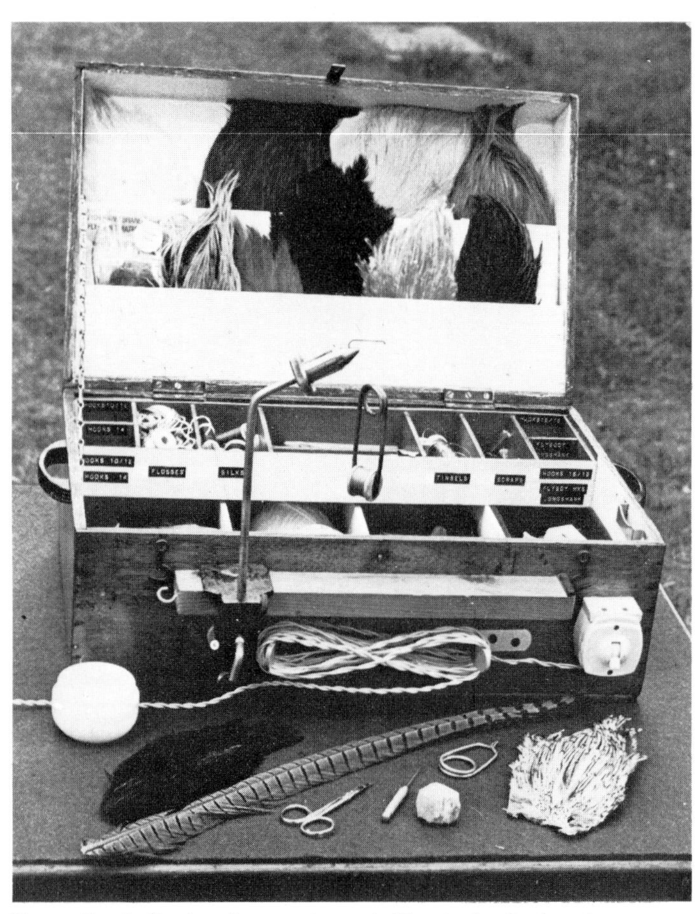

The author's fly-dressing equipment. The tools displayed are wax, bobbin holder, vice, scissors, dubbing needle and hackle pliers. The feathers are black and badger cock capes and a pheasant tail feather.

through it before winding all but the last seven inches back onto the bobbin.

Take the bobbin holder in the right hand and the free end of silk in the left, and, keeping the silk taut between your hands, place it against the shank an eighth of an inch behind the eye of the hook, with the hands positioned as in photo 1. Keeping the left hand still and

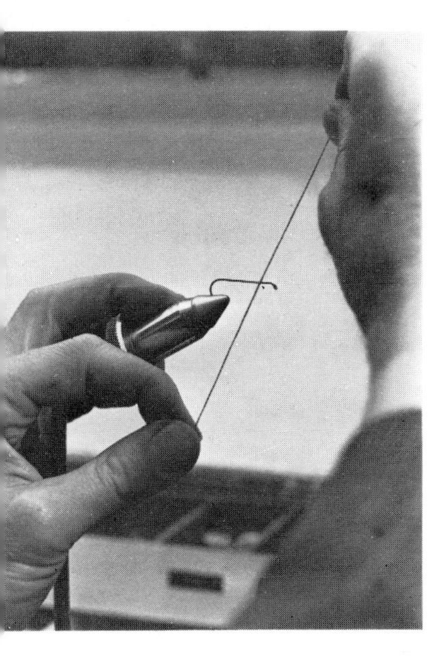

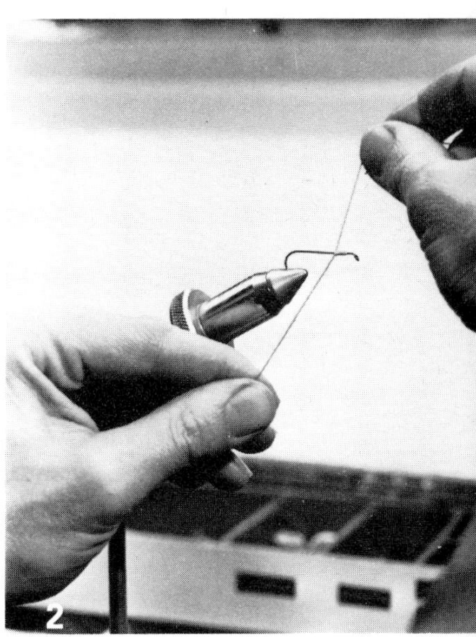
2

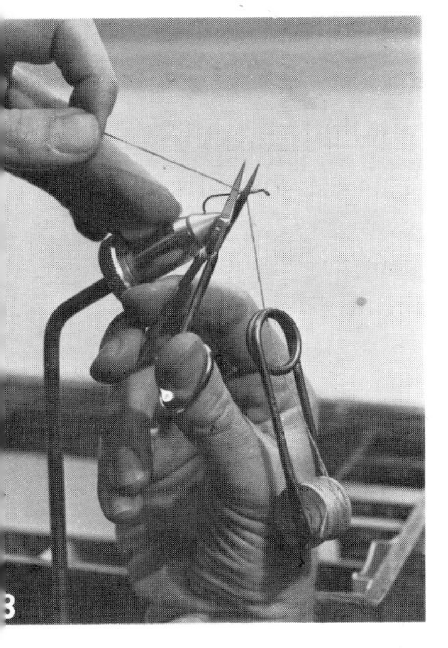
3

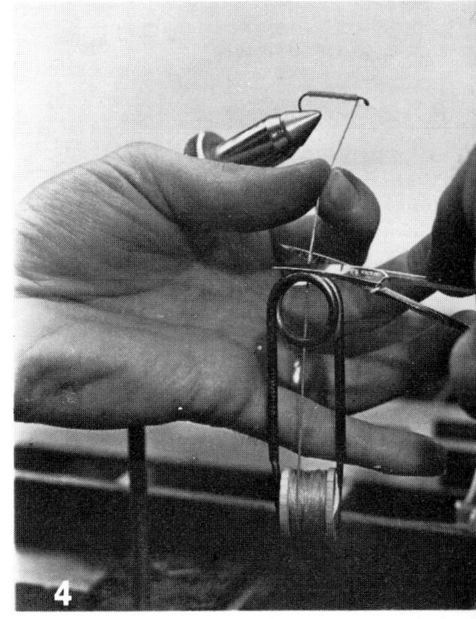
4

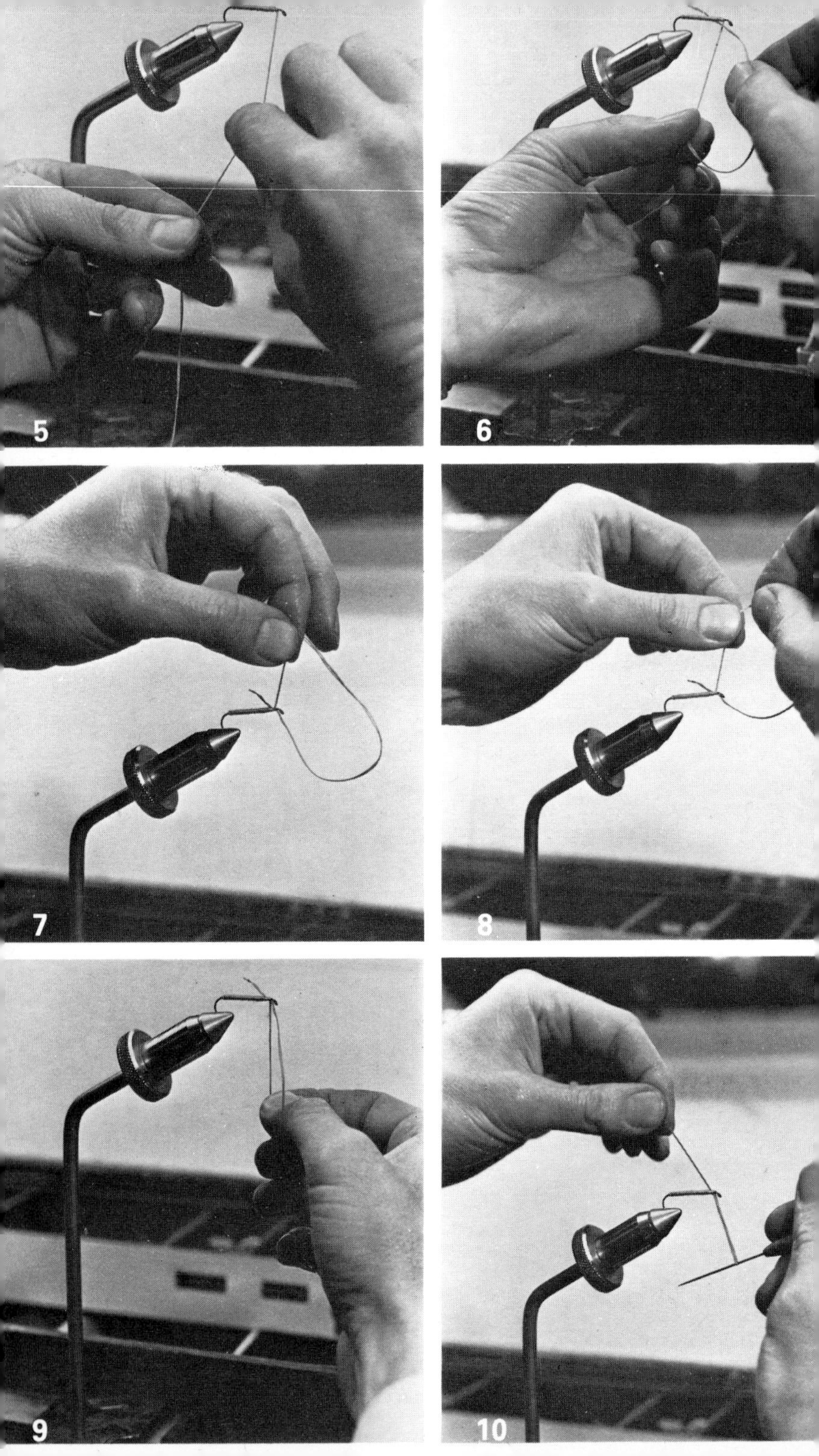
5
6
7
8
9
10

the silk taut take several turns with the right hand around the shank, working towards the bend (photo 2) which will catch-in the free end, trapping it against the shank so that it can be cut off (photo 3). If the bobbin holder is left to dangle while you use the scissors it will keep the silk taut. Go on winding close but not overlapping turns of silk down to the beginning of the bend, and then overlay them with turns back to the eye.

The next operation, whip-finishing, is the most difficult in fly-tying, but once you have mastered it you can start producing real flies. Pull gently on the bobbin holder to lengthen the silk, hold the silk with the left hand, and cut off the bobbin holder beneath it (photo 4). Take hold of the silk with the right thumb and forefinger between the left hand and the hook, *with the back of your right hand facing you* (photo 5). Let go with the left and turn the right over; with well-waxed silk this will make the end of the silk point up towards the hook, and you must slip the free end into the angle between the hook shank and the taut silk (photo 6), making sure the free end is to the left of the taut silk. With the left hand take hold of the taut silk between the right hand and the shank, and, letting go with the right, lift it to catch-in the free end (photo 7). When your left hand is above the hook you can pass the silk into the right to take it down behind the hook (photo 8). In this way, lay on several turns towards the eye, over the free end of silk (photo 9). Then slip the dubbing needle into the loop to hold it taut (photo 10) and pull on the free end, slipping the needle out as the loop closes up. Snip off the end of silk and finish off with a tiny dab of varnish applied with the point of the needle.

DRESSING A HACKLED DRY FLY – GREENWELL'S GLORY

Lay-on with primrose silk and whip down to the bend of a size 14 up-eye hook. Catch in a little bunch of red-game cock hackle fibres *on top* of the shank for the tail, (photo

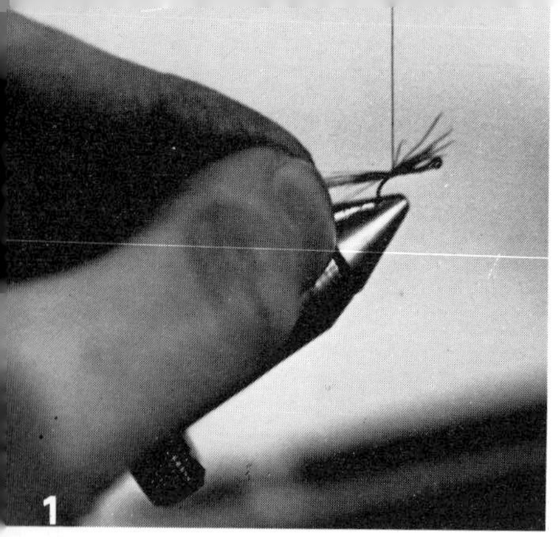

Greenwell's Glory: hackle fibres being caught in at bend to form tail.

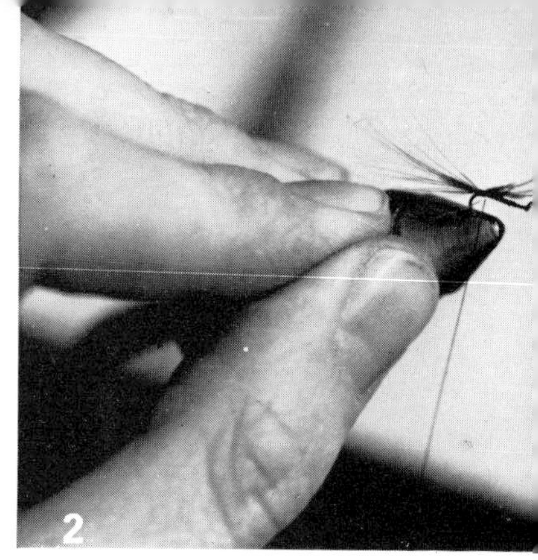

Tying in the wire for the gold rib.

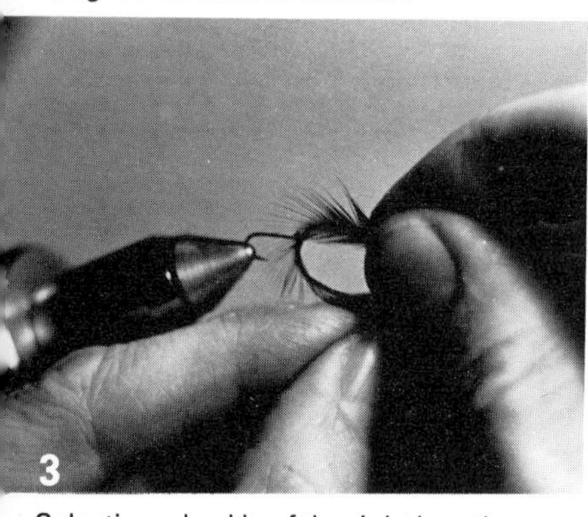

Selecting a hackle of the right length – when the feather is bent the fibres should cover the point of the hook when the stalk is held to the eye.

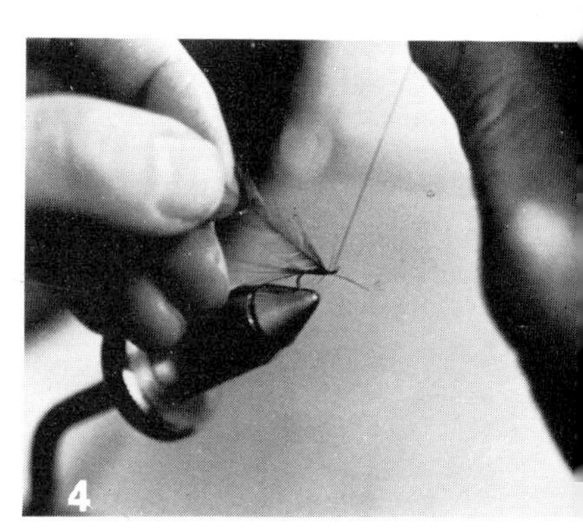

Catching in the hackle

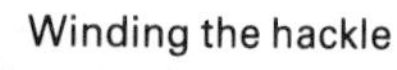

Winding the hackle

Winding the hackle. The silk hangs behind the hackle feather.

The completed fly. For reasons of photographic detail a darker silk than usual has been used.

1) and a length of gold wire underneath for the rib. When tying things in at the tail of any fly, let the end you catch-in be long enough to reach the point where you started laying on as this helps to give the body an even shape. Whip the silk back to where you began, first taking a couple of turns under the hackle fibres to throw them up slightly, then take the gold wire in four turns over the body to the same point (2), tie in the end with two or three turns, and cut off the excess. Take the silk on to the eye in even turns and leave the bobbin holder to hang.

You must now select your hackle; properly it should be a greenwell cock hackle, dark in the centre and red at the edges, but you can use two feathers tied in together, one red-game and one blue-dun. The size is important: the fibres should be the same length as the hook shank and you can check by bending the feather which will make the fibres stand out at right angles to the stalk (photo 3). Strip off the down at the base of the hackle, catch-in the stalk beneath the shank, (photo 4) and tie it down with turns of silk back to where the body ended. Grip the tip of the hackle with the pliers, take four or five turns between the body and the eye, and, leaving the pliers to hang (so holding the hackle tight) wind the silk through the fibres to the eye, securing the tip of the hackle which can be cut off (photo 6). Whip-finish, and the fly is complete (photo 7).

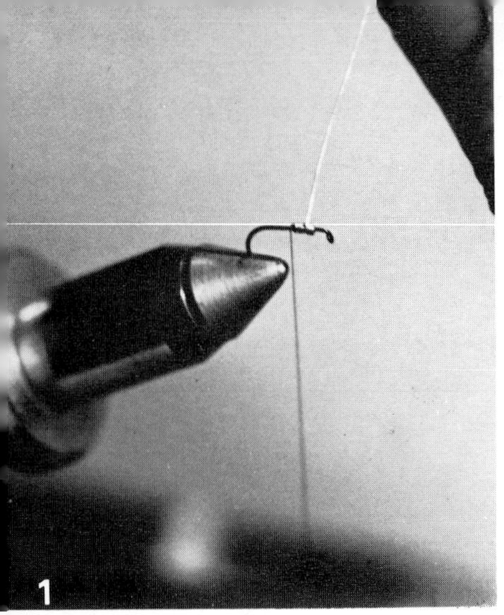

Mold's Olive Nymph: winding on the copper wire.

Catching in the peacock herl.

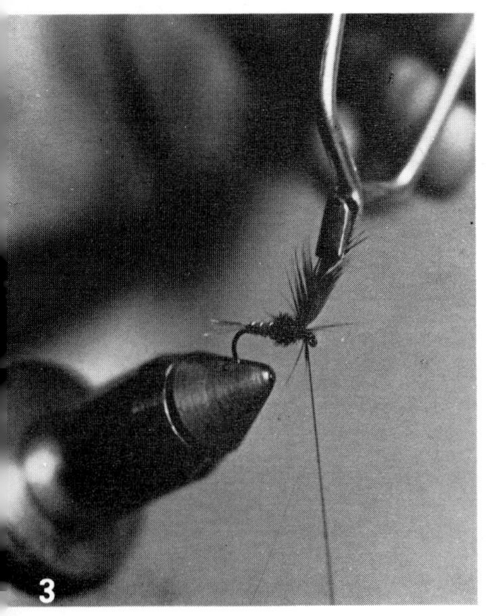

Winding the hen hackle.

The completed fly.

DRESSING A NYMPH – MOLD'S OLIVE NYMPH

In many nymph patterns added weight is used to sink the fly, provided by winding copper wire round the shank at the top of the body to form a bulky thorax (photo 1). Lay-on with black silk and catch in the wire immediately; then take six turns of it towards the eye and five back on top of them and tie the wire off before whipping the silk down to the bend. The body is olive-dyed swan's wing: tie in three fibres from a feather with the pointed ends sticking out a little over the bend for tails, and catch-in some more copper wire for the ribbing. Wind the silk back to the thorax, and cover it with close turns of the swan's feather using the hackle pliers to hold the fibres, ribbing it afterwards with the copper wire. Then tie in a strand of bronze peacock herl (photo 2) and take the silk over the thorax to the eye. Cover the thorax with turns of the peacock herl and tie off in front of the copper 'lump', then tie in a short black hen hackle (photo 3). Take two turns of the hackle, tie it in and whip-finish.

DRESSING A PUPA – THE ORANGE SILVER MIDGE

This is a pattern of my own invention. Lay on with crimson silk and take the whipping half way round the bend of the hook. At the tail catch-in a short length of white wool, a ten inch length of nylon monofilament, a piece of flat silver ribbing and a length of orange-red embroidery cotton (photo 1). Take the silk back to the starting point and form the body with close turns of the cotton closely ribbed with silver. The nylon is whipped on as an overbody to give a translucent effect, and the white wool cut off close for a tail. Then a thorax is dressed from crimson seal's fur which must be dubbed onto the silk: gently pull on the bobbin holder to lengthen it, and apply a little more wax. Take a small

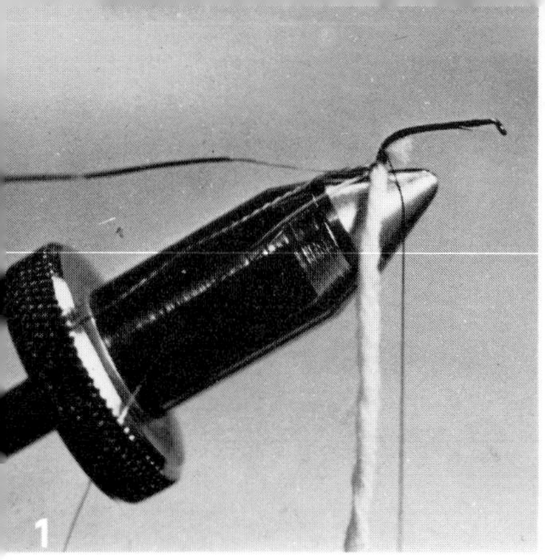

Orange Silver Midge Pupa: body materials tied in at bend. Broad silver rib, red embroidery cotton, nylon monofilament, white knitting yarn, tying silk.

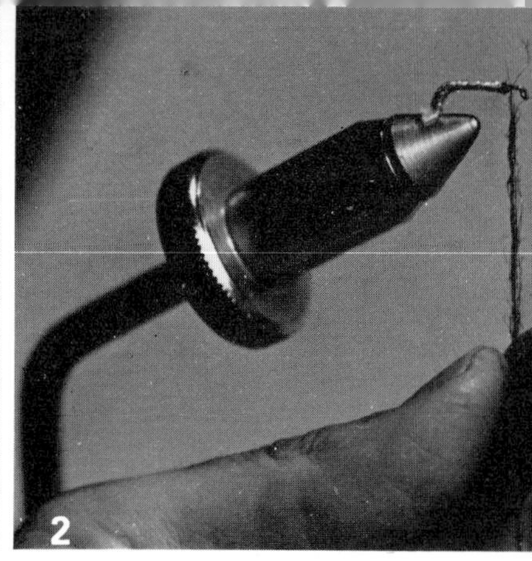

Dubbing on the seal's fur. The silk and fur are being spun between thumb and forefinger.

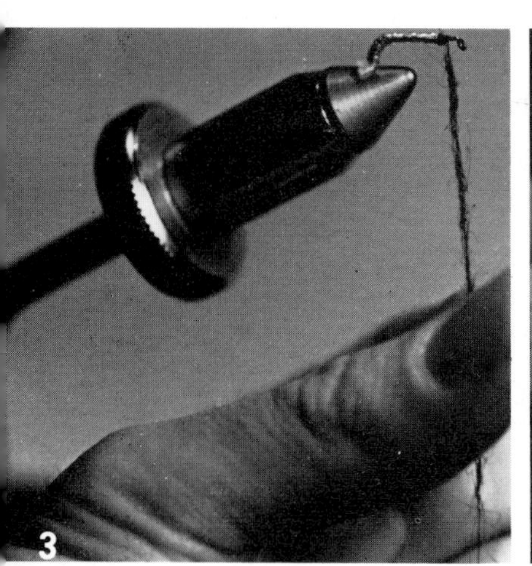

Dubbing on the seal's fur. The movement of the fingers ('spinning' the silk) is here shown completed.

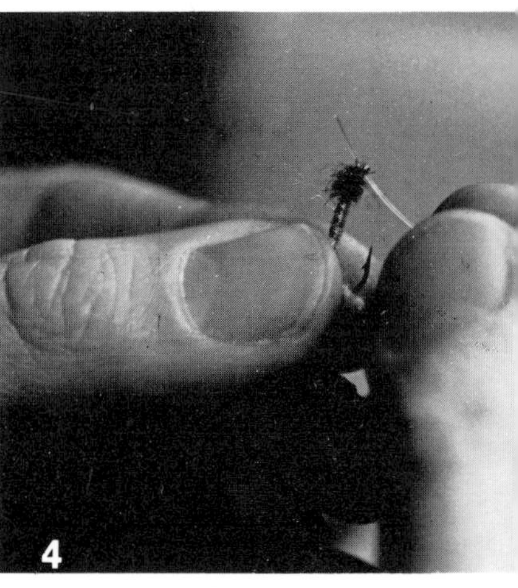

Attaching the completed fly to the leader. The leader-point is passed through the eye from the underside.

pinch of seal's fur and spread it out on the first fingertip of the left hand (photo 2). With the right hand, lay the silk across the fur, and, with the thumb and index finger of the left hand, roll the fur and silk together. It is important to roll only one way, not back and forth, or the

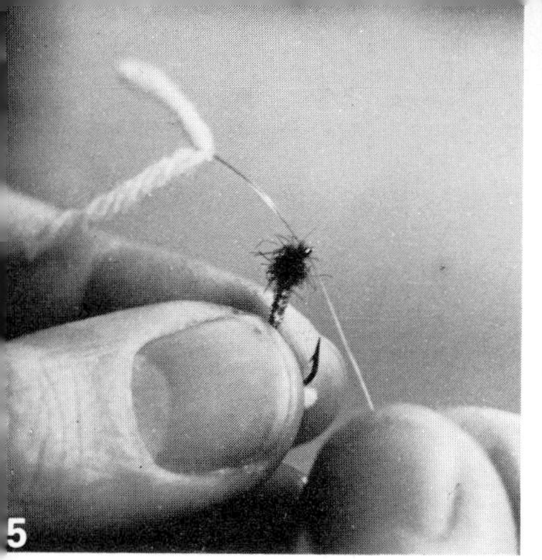

A length of white knitting yarn attached to the point of the leader to form breathing tubes.

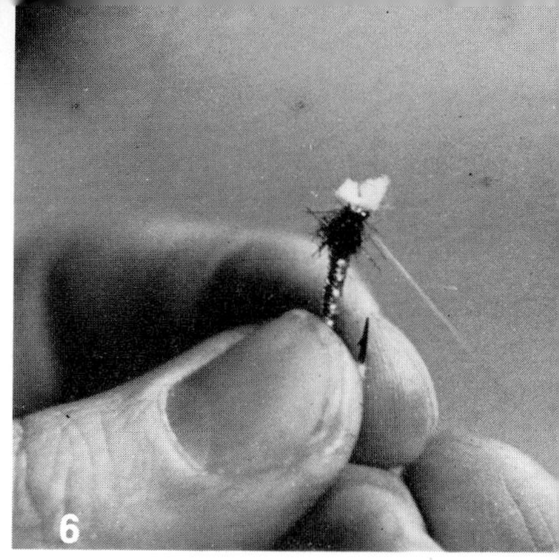

The completed fly with breathing tubes trimmed off short and pulled up against eye of hook. The white fibres of the tail can just be seen between thumb and forefinger.

fur will not stick to the silk. When you have spun the fur onto the silk you simply wind it on above the body to form a thorax, and whip-finish (photo 3).

This fly is not attached to the leader in the usual way (photo 4). Pass the leader point through the eye from the 'wrong' side and fasten it with a double turle knot to a piece of white wool which is then trimmed off close and pulled up against the eye so that it looks like a tiny bow-tie. It catches lake trout for me – it may do the same for you. It will last for ever if you don't lose it, and hold surprisingly big fish.

8 Where to Fish

Books on sports sometimes warn their readers that they cannot expect to master the subject simply by reading about it. While it *is* possible to learn fishing with no other teacher than a book it will always be true that 'it's the fly on the water that catches the trout' as the saying goes: at some time you must put the book down, pick up the rod and go where the trout are. You will certainly come back with a deal of experience to think about. I hope you come back with a trout too, but to help with the thinking I have listed some books for further reading in different categories on p. 95. You can get them from the public library, or start a little fishing library of your own – either way, these are the best books in each branch of the sport.

I hope you will want to go where the fish are as soon as possible but when the time comes to begin, do give yourself every possible advantage; choose the best fishing (which will probably mean the most expensive) within reach of your pocket for your first attempt. Start fishing somewhere where you have at least a good chance of having feeding fish within your limited casting range. In practice that will probably mean avoiding the great public day-ticket reservoirs like Grafham and Chew in favour of the small and sometimes 'exclusive' lakes that are appearing all over the place.

Fisheries in your own area can be found listed in books like *Where to Fish* and *Stillwater Trout Fisheries*, and if you start your fishing at one of these smaller lakes you can begin with confidence that the fish are actually *there.* Only if you have that confidence can you, as a beginner, get on with deceiving them. If you are standing on the shore of what looks like the North Sea, without a rising trout in sight, and waves two feet high, fishing can only become a mindless 'chuck-and-chance-it', and the sort of approach I have been recommending in this book will be impossible. Save the big reservoirs for when you have some experience to work from. Start fishing somewhere where you have at least a chance of success, even if it means fishing less often because it is more expensive. In the end you can only become a successful fly-fisher by catching trout.

BOOK LIST

Lake fishing

C. Voss Bark, *Fishing for Lake Trout with Fly and Nymph* (H. F. & G. Witherby)
B. Clarke, *The Pursuit of Stillwater Trout* (A. & C. Black)

Stream fishing

C. Pearce, *The Confident Fly Fisher* (A. & C. Black)
B. Clarke and J. Goddard, *The Trout and the Fly* (Ernest Benn)
A. Mold, *Presenting the Fly to the Trout*

Fly dressing

C. F. Walker (ed), *The Complete Fly Fisher* (Barrie & Jenkins)
A. Courtney-Williams, *A Dictionary of Trout Flies* (A. & C. Black)
J. Goddard, *Trout Fly Recognition* (A. & C. Black)
J. Goddard, *Trout Flies of Stillwater* (A. & C. Black)

General (every fly fisher should read this)
H. Plunkett-Greene, *Where the Bright Waters Meet*

Index